INTERNAL
MARTIAL ARTS

Michel Chiambretto

Discovery Publisher

Author: Michel Chiambretto
Translator (French to English): Vladimir Markov

616 Corporate Way
Valley Cottage, New York
www.discoverypublisher.com
editors@discoverypublisher.com
Proudly not on Facebook or Twitter

New York • Paris • Dublin • Tokyo • Hong Kong

TABLE OF CONTENTS

INTERNAL
MARTIAL ARTS

Michel Chiambretto

Introduction

The purpose of this guide is to help those who, having explored *the world of martial arts* for many years, are now searching for the so-called "internal" dimension of their practice. Indeed, every martial arts practitioner who has not become a professional in his chosen art, or has not taken a role in its administration, mulls over the objective pursued. With the apprentice's euphoria slowly declining and the desire to become invulnerable vanishing, the aspiration to discover *the hidden dimension* of the practice appears.

It should be made clear from the outset that what will be shown in this book is neither a theory, constructed by synthesizing esoteric texts from Buddhism or Taoism, nor a method, made of random pieces and according to subjective feelings. There are no miracles, nor magic, only a concrete and verifiable approach, as any martial art worthy of its name must deliver.

And here is the rub: nowadays, the so-called "internal" martial arts have become "products" intended for the largest number of people and must, accordingly, be easy to access, promising at the same time health, force, power and sometimes a spiritual dimension available to everyone. Promises also shared by all existing theories resulting from the New Age by the way. So, it is not surprising to see that many *experienced people* in the martial arts smile at such suggestions.

However, even though ease of access does not really exist in the traditional approach, it is true that the proposed internal work allows the discovery of an unexpected dimension inside oneself, or even the expansion of one's own field of consciousness. But to anticipate a future on this kind of path is not really advisable, something that is confirmed by any authentic transmission. How can we conceive something that we have never perceived, other than by relying on overdone images, as mentioned above?

In that case, what can this guide bring to the practitioner? The answer is to indicate a direction to follow, comprised of concrete reference points spread along the path of an ancestral tradition, whose heritage has been transmitted to the present day. Its origin is Far Eastern, but it does not differ in any way, above a certain level of accomplishment, from either Eastern or Western traditions, as I have explained in my previous books. Everything that will be described in the following pages is the result of an experience, which is not only personal, but also that of people who have committed themselves to the Way. A personal experience[1] of half a century of practice with the guidance of knowledgeable *Masters* who, as the Tradition requires, have managed to indicate a path to follow, as well as the use of tools essential to any progress. In this kind of work it is important, and I will try to emphasize this, to know how to take advice from other traditions of the same nature; the purpose is to avoid any notion of community, which can only lead to self-centeredness unsuitable to any evolution. And it is widely known that, in "the world of martial arts", the taste for the exotic is often the common denominator, characterized by a sought-after appearance or even cultural speculation. However, the internal dimension is of an esoteric nature, that is to say hidden, because it is inaccessible to pure reason and also opposed to any trickery. Approaching it can only be done by following a precise path, with traditional tools, and mainly by providing the appropriate instruction.

To that end, and to avoid any misunderstanding, it seems useful to define precisely the notion of "internal".

The confusion between the internal dimension—*Neijia*—and the external one—*Weijia*—is frequent. In China, the origin of this differentiation dates back to either the 16th or 19th century, but it is only an illusion for those unwilling to accept this type of account.

As is often the case, oppositions stem from different interpretations of the same term. According to some, the *internal dimension*

---

1. As a child, school of Judo Kawaishi, fencing, then twenty-five years of intensive practice of Karate, 1st to 4th dan, in Sankukai, Wadoryu, Shotokan, Shitoryu, contact Karate, with knowledgable Masters, such as Y. Nanbu, T. Weber, G. Gruss; 3rd dan in military empty hand combat; in parallel, assistant of many years to Rung, ex-champion of Thai boxing of Lumpinee. After that, twenty-five years of daily practice of an internal martial art, of which ten years of heart-to-heart training — Laoshi Wang XJ, Laoshi Wang SW; without forgetting the seminars of Master H. Plée; the buddhist monk H. M.; the illuminated advice of Wang YS; of L. B-M Yoga Master; Master A. Franceschini; Séverin Batfroi; as well as the Western initiatory tradition.

pertains to all work done with attention on the neuromuscular and the tendinous, that is to say, the "mental gaze" of the practitioner is focused on his physical activity. For others, the association of some more or less sophisticated motor coordination, together with a virtual opposition allowing an isometric muscle action, also relates to this dimension, because it offers the desired external appearance. Finally, for most, the visualization by the practitioner of extreme confrontational situations, but also, antithetically, of states of "wellbeing", can also correspond to the desired convincing aspect.

It is true that the previously mentioned exercises can be useful in terms of combat preparedness, as well as for health or "well-being" improvement. Besides, some modern sports use them successfully in this way. However, the internal dimension that we are going to address here is of a different type and requires a different approach pertaining to both body and mind.

It is a path that allows to find one's *essential nature.* Which, shrouded by a set of conditionings, allows us to be in touch with what all traditions recognize as the shared "substance", or "breath" if you will — *Qi, Ki, Prana, Pneuma, Ruah, Ruh, Spiritus* — a "substance" that, in the martial arts, allows the practitioner to transcend himself and exceed his limits, not only physically, but also on the level of his consciousness.

Of course, this assertion may vex the reader, same as most practitioners of the internal arts have been in the beginning of a singular practice.

Nevertheless, there is no miracle, nor myth, only an authentic tradition, the likes of which can be found anywhere around the world. This one has had a martial usage for survival. But others, like Yoga in India, Taoism in China, Sufism in the East, Gnosis in the West, have had purely initiatory functions while using similar tools. Yet, as proven by numerous examples, the line between the two aspects becomes blurred, to say the least, as time goes on.

Also, this kind of practice will have at its base work in awareness of a so-called "profound" dimension, which escapes by its nature usual understanding. "Vanity!", one may think, but in fact the fruit of a tradition where each heir is but a link. Furthermore, contrary to any creation or compilation, it could be said, same as stated by

Confucius, "I am only transmitting without creating anything of my own", all credit going to the ancient Masters.

In addition, it is worth indicating the most important point, something I will not fail to repeat, because it is fundamental.

To be able to access this "profound nature", it is necessary to resort to a true "reeducation" of the motor function and, to do that, of the sensory perception. To address this issue I will not use a theoretical approach but rather, as the tradition wants it, an empirical one. The objective is to penetrate the principles to apply, the ones that have been bequeathed to us to activate a dimension of awareness that is today asleep. The mistake, as already mentioned, would be to develop a sophisticated theory, which only specializing scientists will be able to eventually acknowledge, or to make a synthesis of Buddhist and Taoist texts available to everyone. Which is nevertheless quite common.

And it is often here, as we will see, where the pitfall lies. To be comfortable in its choices and actions our rational mind needs to intellectualize the logic of the method used. Which is true in the sports today, where the scientific analysis has become an essential support to every federation, but is also becoming true for the field of martial arts. Arts like aikido are rationalized with catalogued techniques, precise, defined by diagrams, while the internal work of visualization, of intention, has disappeared, except in rare cases. Other arts approach the notions of Qi with anatomical atlases, explanations from Chinese medicine, "energy" centers, a thousand times cited and taken up in theoretical compilation works. Hence, it is easy to understand the rejection of such speculative explanations by experimented practitioners.

Another pitfall is just as common: the interpretation of the tools being shared. It is indeed surprising to see that followers of authentic Masters express the teaching received in contradictory ways. Some develop the heritage completely rationally, while others, coming from the same source, venture into abstractions that are difficult to comprehend. In the same way, in practice it is possible to see sports intended for the largest number of people and, in parallel, very discreet, to say the least, expressions of supra-sensory dimensions. Of course, as always, each side claims to be the only heir to the tradition in question.

The conclusion, which seems obvious, is that the recipient will only develop what his profound nature allows him to, something we will address together.

For those who feel the need for it, my intention in this book will be to bring clarity on the essence itself of the internal arts, with the caveat that anything written can never replace a heart-to-heart exchange with a teacher of the Tradition.

Nevertheless, this guide can indicate a direction to follow at a given time.

My Thanks

Claudine, Marie, Paul, Thomas; Séverin Batfroi for his precious help, Éric Maton for the Aikido; Henri, Dinh, Yoshinao, Gilbert, Rung, Heinrich, Tamas, Ming, Xuan Jie, Shang Wen, Howe Man, Yi Shen, Henry, Antoine, Lucien, Jean-Paul, Didier, Claude, Gérard; without forgetting all the members of the Kong jin association.

DISCLAIMER

The author and the publisher are not responsible for any injury resulting from the practice of instructions included in this book. The described activities, physical or other, could be tiresome or dangerous for certain individuals and so the reader should consult a medical professional beforehand.

The author and the publisher do not recommend nor approve self-treatment by laymen in this matter, and cannot be held responsible for treatments done on the basis of information contained in this book.

The martial dimension

The martial arts have as their objective, theoretically, to prepare the practitioner for a future confrontation. To prepare him not only physically but also and more importantly, mentally.

At the origins of most martial arts schools, Chinese or Japanese, we find military men such as the mythical general Yue Fei, warriors like Miyamoto Musashi or Takeda Sokaku, caravan guards like Ji Jike or Guo Yunshen, as well as civilians forced to defend themselves in a world where death was never far away.

It is not surprising then that the search for effectiveness was the main goal of practitioners in ancient times. The shadow of death was following them at every step.

Keeping that in mind, it can be said that today's martial arts practitioners, from the beginner to the expert, are, at the least, far removed from this type of reality. Knowing that tomorrow will be your last day gives an awareness of the practice that no visualization or codified combat can replace. Its daily repetition, year after year, leaves an indelible mark upon people's mind.[1]

---

1. The fact that I have spent time with a grand-father who participated in the Great War, and more particularly the Chemin des Dames, and a father combatant in the Vercors and then in the Tabors, during the German campaign, allows me to make this affirmation.

Then, is it surprising that these "ancients", to bear the unbearable, have gone on to search in the midst of spiritual practices the acceptance of the notion of imminent death? Perhaps, it was during their meetings and work with Taoism, Buddhism and Shamanism, that they have discovered not only the awareness, which would have allowed them to accept dying at any moment, but also an increased martial ability?

The tool of spiritual awakening thus becoming a martial tool, an evidence-based paradox.

Are these tools the fruit of the primordial Tradition, coming from the origin of man, when his perception and his consciousness were still awake, a tradition that existed from East to West? It is possible to believe that, as I will elaborate on these pages, and as I have explained in my previous books.

However, every theoretical development requires a more concrete support, and particularly so when talking about the martial aspect.

The support I have chosen is an allegory. It will allow the reader to avoid any particular susceptibility to the subject matter.

Imagine men from some primitive tribe. To fetch their food, they have to regularly cross a precipice. To do that, they have to walk on a very narrow wooden beam and risk their lives at every step. The accidents abound and in turn volunteers are becoming rare, a critical issue.

So, in order to create vocations, the old sages of this tribe decide to prepare novices for the trial, in a way that exalts their solidarity.

With this goal in mind, they plan a training in several stages.

The first one is to make the apprentices walk on flat ground, while following a drawn rectangle symbolizing the beam. They are taught to make one step after another, without hurry, arms outstretched to maintain their balance, eyes on the objective.

They will be made to repeat the exercise day after day with the most restraint possible.

Over time, however, an entire group of people formalizes this practice, declaring that in its teaching lies the truth of the ultimate stage. Which is not wrong, it must be said. They then decide to create a school based uniquely on the precepts of this stage. Pleasant and allowing them to have a friendly activity.

Others, part of the same group and desiring to evolve their practice, develop acrobatics from the same bases, which, even though useless, allow them to compare themselves to each other without any risk. The spectacular aspect is very attractive.

Finally, a third part of the group, sensing that the final trial is what calls into question the actual essence of Man, bonds with the shaman of the tribe. Together with him, they learn the tools to free themselves from the "bubble of individual consciousness" and to reunite with the undivided consciousness. They keep the core work but also add to it the teachings of the shaman. Over time, they end up forgetting the final trial, the objective becoming spiritual.

The second stage is more concrete and the future equilibrists are made to walk on a beam 30 centimeters above the ground. There is a risk, but only minimal. At worst, they would sprain an ankle. Which could scare a few. Same techniques, same principles.

In the same way as previously described another group decides to stop at this stage and formalize it. They know how to stay sober-minded and also search for the essence of the ultimate trial.

With the same desire to evolve, others develop acrobatics that are useless, but fun and demonstrative.

The only comment to be made here is that, in both cases, the adherents give themselves the appearance of being used to the precipice. A very human egotistic attitude.

Following the progression, the third stage puts the beam at one meter above the ground. The risk is bigger. If they fall, they could break an arm, a leg, maybe get knocked out; and this, even though there is a foam mat on the ground.

Some, arriving at this stage, think that it must be generalized as it allows, without a huge risk, to get closer to the ultimate trial. The bravest, without being reckless, follow this tendency but, same as the ones before, refuse to proceed onto the next stage.

Following the logic, those who want stronger sensations or to show off add impressive acrobatics. It is all very appealing.

The followers of these two trends, same as the ones before, give themselves the appearance of being used to the precipice.

The fourth stage is reserved for those who, having went through the previous ones, want to anticipate the feel of the final trial. It is true that the "dominant male" or "alpha male" side compels them to make this choice.

The beam is placed three meters above the ground. Every fall will lead to either an injury or a knock out and, in a few cases, to serious short and mid-term consequences. The trial is psychologically difficult.

> *Seeing an opportunity to profit financially, a few shameless elders decide to exploit human nature. The part of this nature that enjoys the risk taken by others without exposing oneself to it, i.e., being a spectator to the risk taken by others.*
>
> *Thus, the elders recruit and manage to convince some to place themselves in danger for the pleasure of others. This way they create shows based on the principles of this stage in the neighboring tribes. The more there are falls and injuries, the more there are spectators and profits. For the protagonists taking risks for the pleasure of others is not easy. So, to gain some courage, a few use the benefits of certain plants. An understandable attitude.*

Finally, there is the end of the preparation, the objective, which is to walk day after day across the beam above the bottomless abyss, this giving the impression of it sucking in every tiny person who is passing.

Those who have managed to make their balance natural, who can advance without hesitation, without thinking, with restraint in their movements, who can ignore the bottomless abyss that can swallow them in a terrifying absolute, who can forget themselves day after day, complete the trial. Of course, the wind, the rain, a passing weakness, can all provoke a fatal error, but they know this and accept it.

> *Note that, as mentioned above, some have stopped at the previous stages and are not part of this final group.*

Others, however, react differently when facing the trial, even though they have overcome the previous stages without issues.

The following behaviors can be observed:

- Those who, refusing to cross, run in the opposite direction. An instinctive form of wisdom?
- Those who stall, frozen by fear, unable to take a single step, but also incapable of fleeing.

This last case obviously corresponds to the inhibition that can strike any individual. Something also true for those passing the trial every day, as they can become victims of such mental blocks at any time.

It should be noted that, for the individuals who have completed the trial in extreme conditions, a storm of wind and rain, where everything becomes uncertain, where at every moment a gust can blow them away, this crossing is like a "black hole". The "lizard brain" takes over, no thinking, a spontaneous instinctive action to survive, which will not leave any memory other than a few elusive images.

What can be seen in those people who cross the precipice by necessity, is that they do not take pride in it, nor do they have any pretense — though there are exceptions, as always.

What do they want? Well, for a footbridge to be made so they would not need to risk their lives anymore and, above all, subsequently, the lives of their children. It can be observed that they have lost any desire to brag about the subject, contrary to what they have been doing in the previous stages, with friends and close ones having often perished at their side.

Let us end here this allegory.

The readers would have without doubt made the connection with their own practice and placed themselves on the progression ladder described. To facilitate reading, I have allowed myself, as you have noticed, to develop the stages in the martial arts in a colorful diatribe.

However, it is not my intention to criticize the scale of values of this or that practice.

At ground level, the artistic expression can exist. So can a choice involving work on concentration and motor control, or else leisure, mental relaxation and a place to meet friends, passionate about the same activity. Nothing to blame, on the contrary. These can also be a Path to spiritual realization.

At one to three meters above the ground courage is needed to measure oneself against the risk or the other person. But these experiences cannot be compared to that of the ultimate decision.

Indeed, does anyone believe that "someone who wins a championship with his bamboo sword" will succeed in defeating the same adversaries in a real situation where any mistake is to be paid with one's life?

Nothing is less certain, as the situation does not require the same fundamental resources of the human being, nor the same martial arts techniques—any fantasy, any aesthetic or theoretical aspect is out of place.

Nevertheless, a characteristic of the martial art is, and must be, to surpass oneself at a given moment. The tools used in these arts have as their objective the improvement of both mind and body. Just like the sculptor working the stone to extract his artwork, the martial artist must work on himself. And if, in a similar way, he can and must sublimate his at a given moment, it is essential for him to go through concrete steps. Steps that will help to avoid any illusory pretense.

Therefore, the practitioner can be advised to carry out a friendly encounter at "30 centimeters" or "one meter" above the ground, but especially by coming out of his *microcosm*. Of course, it is necessary to have some experience in the art beforehand.

To do that, my advice is:

- Choose an opponent who is "rustic", doing manual labor—therefore acting naturally and spontaneously;
- Afterwards, to test the kung fu, the level of accomplishment, without brutality but "vigorously".

This type of opponent will allow you to avoid the predictable reactions of the practitioners of your own art and, above all, the "synchronicity"—and will, perhaps, allow you to question your own conditioning.

By synchronicity, I mean the programmed, achieved by repetition, reaction to a stimuli. The stimuli being the execution by one of the practitioners of a "given set of techniques", which instantly brings about in the other a "conditioned reaction". Irrelevant of whether this set of techniques is "effective" or not.

The most obvious examples:

- In modern aikido, one learns to fall at the slightest touch. In fact, reproducing the same "scenario" is enough to provoke the fall. It can sometimes even be seen that the fall precedes any action;

- In karate, bunkai of kata — the implementation of techniques corresponding to some of its phases — are often unrealistic;

- There is also the formal tuishou[1], which can equally lead to the same phenomenon of "synchronicity" — not to be confused with voluntary work in "harmony".

Tuishous based solely on pushing and thrusting, while the practitioners remain vulnerable to a blow, are a pure martial heresy. Not to mention the "fixed step" where the practitioners are not supposed to move around at all.

But the aberrations are numerous, including in the so-called combat sports. Doing ground work while talking about an "ultimate fight", where twisting, biting and tearing are forbidden, as well as any attack against the eyes or the genitals, probably is not really accurate. The same when standing. But we are drifting away from the perspective of working on oneself and the notion of art.

Remaining in the "patterns of physical activity" where each and everyone is conditioned the same way can only lead to many martial disillusions.

Also, in the internal arts, this type of friendly encounter might avoid you to be in the same company as those who feel the "energy" inside themselves, or sense the "fields of energy", or some other subjective phenomenon. Mainly, it allows to consciously "substantiate" the "substance" inside you and its use — something I will develop subsequently — that is to say, the pragmatic aspect of your practice.

Even if it means, depending on your wishes, taking a path out-

---

1. See chapter "Pushing hands".

side of the martial arts. But this phase is necessary, so as to be under no "illusion".

Let us get back to our allegory.

Why did I develop it in the form of a diatribe?

Simply because we must be honest with ourselves and, possibly, with the others. I admit, as without doubt you do, smiling at the fierce warrior contrivance of some martial arts experts who have never known a real confrontation.

Additionally, the allegory allows to readjust one's practice. Talking about combat, have we tried it on the ground, at 30 centimeters above the ground, at one meter, at three, above the abyss? And, consequently, what is the conclusion that can be made?

Conversely, we can, with time passing and thanks to an authentic practice, realize that the notion of "art" in martial arts has not been misused. On the condition, of course, that we have found the tools that allow the individual to accomplish himself after working with them for years.

On this, we should also be sincere and precise. What is meant by "accomplishment" or, if you prefer, the "Way" — *Dao or Do*?

Firstly, we should put aside everything that is common to many fields. This is to say: what are we searching for precisely?

• To become stronger and more powerful?

But, as one Japanese Master was saying: "A gorilla is stronger than a man, but who wants to be a gorilla?" — **Although some might answer: "Me!"**...

• To become the dominant male, to seduce the female?

Why not, but this desire diminishes with age.

• Exercise power over a microcosm?

This is natural for our mammalian brain.

• To be loved or even worshipped?

An obvious need of the heart.

• Make money?

Essential in our society. Also, everything that is free loses its value in the eyes of our contemporaries.

- To play the wise man from fairy tales and legends, to adorn oneself with mysterious powers?

A comfortable situation, because it allows to remain in the dreams of childhood.

- To forget one's own fear of nothingness, synonymous with the deadly disease that is life?

So common!

- A bit of everything?

But we should focus on the more essential:

- To be able to defend oneself from a potential aggression?

This is the vocation of the martial arts and the development of your inner force will allow you to go beyond your physical ability. Unfortunately—**or fortunately**—same as you will always find someone weaker, you will always find someone stronger.

However, surpassing oneself is already an achievement.

- To live a passion and use the tools offered by the practice to calm down the inner fire that consumes one's being?

This can be found in some internal martial arts. Yet, it is necessary to feel the need for it. This need, or lack of it, explains without doubt the different paths extant in every style of the internal martial arts.

You are the sculptor but also the artwork.

In the end, it must be emphasized that this internal work allows some practitioners to broaden their field of consciousness. We will see how.

The "proper" approach to the internal arts

It is very difficult to communicate a personal experience. Not for a lack of words but because no sensitive state can fit into language. Additionally, depending on each person, on their age, life, culture, history, each word will have a different meaning and will draw a different picture. This is certainly why every transmission has lead to various interpretations. This is not inconsequential!

However, what is true for this notion of experience is also true for every transmission and thus for those relating to the internal arts.

That is why I think it is imperative to begin elaborating, after the martial dimension, common to all related arts, on the notion of "understanding". The latter will explain the discrepancies, or even oppositions, which exist in trends that share the same source.

Let us begin with a quote:

Master Wang Xuanjie stated that "the talent of a practitioner does not depend on time spent training, nor on his efforts, nor on his seniority. Neither does it depend on his health, age, or methods, and even less so on the slowness or quickness of his movements, but on the degree of understanding of the principles that he has[1]".

As always, the difficulty to penetrate the meaning of a quote lies in the context of the author and his willingness to transmit. Master Wang Xuanjie, like some of the authentic Masters from the past and rare contemporaries, was an expert in hiding a large number of key elements of the practice both in his writing and in his imagery — this is frequent in initiatory teaching; it can even be said that it is part of the pedagogy, because it allows to separate the wheat from the chaff. However, his level of kung fu could only leave speechless those who had the chance to know him. But periodically, he would, a little at a time, give precious advice like the one above.

1. Wang Xuanjie, *Dachengquan*.

In keeping with the willingness to go beyond any theory, we should avoid analyzing the etymology of the words in that quote, and rather try to find the relevant historical examples in the martial arts that confirm it.

First and foremost, an observation. The so-called authentic heirs of Masters of esoteric traditions or internal arts have developed schools that are quite disparate.

Aikido can be used as a reference, an art of great quality, transformed in an "internal" Way by its creator O'Sensei Ueshiba, himself heir of Sokaku Takeda of Daitoryu, a martial method of great effectiveness.

The O'Sensei had many disciples, but his succession was characterized by various and sometimes antithetical interpretations.

To quote two obvious examples:

- The one of Master Shioda who understood the esoteric aspect of the teaching and developed a surprising personal Ki, while remaining very pragmatic when teaching in law enforcement;
- The one of Master Tomiki, excellent practitioner, who used the knowledge of his art to create a competitive sport, corresponding to the ambitions of the modern world.

But even more surprising are the answers of those two heirs to the question about O'Sensei's prodigious abilities. They do show the origin of the notable difference existing between their respective approaches.

While Sensei Shioda speaks of:

"A spiritual force that is a reality",[1]

Sensei Tomiki states that to him:

"This is a matter of muscular training which is part of modern physical education. It is called isometrics. That is to say, we can train inner or outer groups of muscles by pushing or **pulling**."[2]

Note that, context-wise, at the time, teaching was more about showing than explaining:

"When we were training, Ueshiba Sensei would make us feel

1. Stanley Pranin, *Aikido Pioneers — Prewar Era.* Collection of interviews.
2. Ibid.

things directly rather than teach us... We had to think about things by ourselves... And now, I continue to do what I have been able to put together."[1]

It can be seen that although based on a common teaching, the actual understanding can differ. Of course, a few cynics might say that one has received a more advanced training than the other. To that, it is possible to reply that the direction shown by O'Sensei was the same.

Morihei Ueshiba, aware of the lack of understanding of the Way he wanted to transmit, made the following remark in the last years of his life:

"I have given my life to opening the path of Aikido but when I look back no one is following me."[2]

Which tends to prove that the same presence, the same actions, the same words, can be interpreted in different, even opposite, ways by every witness or student.

This can also be true for oneself. **Often, too often, the lack of satisfaction with one's own progress leads to blaming the tools, or the pseudo-inability of the teacher, but rarely oneself, one's own lack of understanding**.

The understanding of the principles, of the tools, comes through a "correct state of awareness". From experience, it can be clarified that individual nature plays a fundamental part. Every outcome of listening is often the fruit of our own conditioning, culture, personal evolution — I will address this again in the theory of the triune brain by MacLean.

On this topic, is it any wonder that, amongst the most accomplished Masters, some were either fragile children in bad health or people who had suffered traumatic experiences — reality or metaphor?

Consequently, it can be inferred that their sensitivity threshold was lowered to such a level, that, in response, their intuitive perception was exacerbated beyond the common standard.

Another significant example is the art of yi quan or dacheng quan,

---

1. Ibid.

2. John Stevens, *Invincible Warrior*.

which only recently rose from anonymity in the West.

In this school, whose *founder* is Master Wang Xiangzhai, most contemporary experts work with a strong internal physical tension based on micro-movements. In contrast, a few very rare exceptions are in total relaxation, supported by obvious, and above all verifiable, density.

The marked contrast should raise questions about this divergence and its origin. But, as it is the same lineage, the adherents do not seem to think about it.

It should be noted that the *founder* of this school made clear in his writing that a practitioner should avoid any "illusion". A term that can only create confusion in the minds of disciples of both yesterday and today. However, there is an important factor that should be taken into account in the analysis of the Master's writing: the context of the political period. It was necessary to negate any abstraction stemming from the ancestral Tradition. The choice to call, for a time, his school "Quan Xue"—boxing science—is probably due to these same circumstances. And, to think that everything can be said in a text, is to not take into account the Chinese martial tradition. The latter not only did not divulge secrets easily, but also knew how to skillfully disinform. Yet, evidently, work such as the use of sound, "Shi sheng"—testing the sound—specific to this school, cannot have a physical support. Which should indicate a direction for the followers of this art. However, in an identical manner, the sound "Kiai"—uniting the breath—of the Japanese martial arts, has also lost any "substance".

How to explain then this notable difference in the practice?

Is individual choice at the origin of the refusal of some adherents of any notion of Qi in their practice? Or, did the heritage differ, with variable levels of teaching? Or else, the individual's own nature? Or a little bit of everything?

With these explanations, the idea is not to disparage this or that expert, or to create useless polemics, but rather to clarify that, depending on the understanding, the paths can diverge, because resting on different principles. Which does not take away from anyone's martial qualities.

Another factor in the lack of comprehension of the internal dimension of the martial arts may be the deterioration resulting from social evolution. **Today, the various martial arts have become "products" aimed at the largest number of people.** Thousands of teachers live thanks to their teaching. So, clearly, it has become necessary to offer "arts" that are easily accessible, pleasant, fun, rewarding and consequently rarely effective.

The issue with these arts is related to their "success". Going back to the metaphor of the source, i.e., a discreet transfer of knowledge from Master to disciples, the schools have now literally become streams with thousands of teachers dragging after themselves millions of students. The consequences are many and they concern said transfer of knowledge.

Let us consider two examples:

1. Today, modern aikido offers technical charts and a rational process, having lost, more or less, the notion of Yi, and the notion of Ki has become a purely philosophical theory.

   What has happened to the communion with the Kami of the trees of O'Sensei — Kami, or spirit, or spiritus, or "breath"?

   Who still remembers the Yi and the work with Ki in the rowing exercise, Fune Kogi Undo? What has happened to the progressive development of Yi/Ki with the use of sound Kotodama — word- soul — or of Norito — incantations for purification in Shinto — other than only to repeat the audible illusion? The list would be long.

   Nevertheless, current aikido, even if moving away from its source, answers perfectly the demands of most followers.

2. Contemporary taiji is, with rare exceptions, but a school of soft gymnastics. Every movement is a copy of the ideal image of the Master or teacher, with the theory of Qi for support.

   This activity moves away from the origins of the internal martial arts, yet is appreciated by a large majority of practitioners for its "wellbeing" aspect. There is nothing much to say, as the result is in line with the desire.

   Outside the martial context the most obvious example is yoga. An initiatory art par excellence, which has become nothing but a fun and trendy activity.

But honestly, would it be possible to sell these internal arts by telling the truth?

That is to say, to explain that only after three years of tedious practice, alone, from one to three hours a day, you can consider yourself as an apprentice? Which then allows you to train for another five to seven years in the same rigorous manner to finally become a companion and be able to really start training.

Not easy to sell, right? How many clients would we find?

The desire for commercialization is omnipresent in our society and here we can also mention the external martial arts, or other initiatory Ways such as Taoism, Zen, calligraphy etc.

This slide toward commercialism, at least in the eyes of the enthusiasts, is it wanted by the leaders of the official bodies? Is it the consequence of a sales system made for the largest number of people? Is it the result of social evolution? Is it a consequence of the action of "memes" in Richard Dawkins' theory?[1]

To each their own answer.

For those who want to find the essence of their internal art, and the understanding necessary for any progression, **it is necessary at some point to separate "the container from the content"**.

How should this "container" be understood? Everything that varies between the different martial or even spiritual teachings. Whether the form, the techniques, the appearance, the rites, the history, the erudition, or the folklore, the fairy tales and the legends that amateurs of exoticism enjoy so much.

To put it simply, everything that serves as a reference today.

What about the "content"?

There are two types of content:

1. Firstly, the principles of the "body" — and not the techniques that use them. The synergy of mass and segments, the wholeness, the potential timing offsets. All of this must become "natural" over time — "everything I do is technique": Morihei Ueshiba. In a confrontation, the principles must be already acquired, applied by instinct, and as to the techniques, they should be adapted to the situation, that is to say, non-conventional. There is often a

---

1. Richard Dawkins, *The Selfish Gene*.

confusion between the two. Someone who does not understand would want to learn a multitude of techniques, while forgetting the principles;

2. Furthermore, in the internal arts it should be taken into account what the most important aspect is, namely, mental work — *Yi, Jingshen* — and what it allows to use — the *Qi*. This is the actual purpose of the work done, something not always visible to the uninitiated eye.

Obviously, as with any physical activity, it is possible to add the taste for effort, will, discipline, decisiveness and sometimes "a healthy mind in a healthy body".

The confusion between superficial and essential is often due to the non-differentiation of container and content. But, conversely, it should be noted that the superficial is more visible and more tangible, while the essential is more obscure and more abstract for the uninitiated.

However, is that all?

No, there is an obstacle, and not a small one, which has to be kept in mind.

As a matter of fact, all Traditions consider it **our biggest enemy,** described in all initiations, **namely one's own self**.

You want to connect consciously to the "object", but how to "understand" what is to be done, if every day you are small-minded, petty, limited, a symbol of omnipresent self-centeredness?

To understand is in fact to yield to the principle, be it a direction, an Yi, a Qi. This principle must invade not only every part of your body, but also your mind. So:

- If you are preoccupied with your appearance, your image, during practice, how can you have self-insight?

- If you only want personal gain, how to expand your consciousness?

- Not to mention the contemporary trend, contagious to say the least, of the practitioner showing off through various communication mediums;

To understand is also to be in the "proper state" during practice and to maintain it afterwards, as long as possible. That is to say, to maintain this state in *everyday life,* which means to be in harmony with the foundational principles of your art while you go about your everyday activities — family life, free time and, less obvious, work.

Practicing with "Yi" in relaxation, as an induction, requires a calm mind and is logically opposed to any everyday action inducing agitation or mental and muscular tension.

Strength and weight training are equally to be proscribed, and tuishou work with strong resistance — before the kung fu is actually present — is not desirable. All of these can only work against the ongoing metamorphosis. Holding onto activities that rely on physical and mental habits from your childhood will only bring your reeducation to a *standstill.* An obvious, yet continuing problem, stemming from a lack of understanding.

To understand is also to question your work "routine" of techniques. **There is a confusion between quantity and quality**. Whether alone or in a group.

Most of the time students, during a given training, are happy when they are tired or even exhausted. Smiling, pleased with themselves, they congratulate each other with expressions such as "We did well!". But what they should understand is that the reason why they are following a teaching is to "learn and therefore understand" and not to repeat "empty" exercises, even though some complexity is being added. Often, said complexity refers to a set of movements or situations, but without a detailed explanation of body and mind principles. To the initiated, the most surprising is that questions about the essentials do not even come to mind to the students.

The reason for this passive role is without a doubt how the student situates himself. Whether by the will of the teacher or not, of the system, of the school, or of the student himself, the latter is subjected to and *tails* the teacher. He expects passively the understanding of the practice and, consequently, his own progression.

The internal arts are of a different nature. **According to the Tradition, the Master points the way, the tools, the principles, but it is the disciple who has to take care of himself**. He must, through good questions or remarks, obtain the correct information. He must also see "with his heart" the practice of the Master and perceive through empathy.

The "routine" is also to watch a senior practice and think "I know this", a classic mistake. The right attitude would be to act the exact opposite way. **You must, similar to when your heart makes you see a close person absent for a very long time, "rediscover each and every time" what is being done.** If this becomes "natural", then you can only be surprised. The body principles that have not been revealed are often "visible" this way! And many other things too.

Lastly, one more thing to consider. It concerns the **"heart-to-heart" teaching. This is an empathic relationship between Master and student, where the communion of minds allows to forego discursiveness, and where gestural and sensible expressions are sufficient to communicate the essentials.** In this regard, try to put yourself in the teacher's shoes. It has taken him years to learn what he knows, tens of years to understand with both mind and body. Do you think that the trainee, by paying a certain amount, or by jumping from one teacher to another, as it is common nowadays, will be able to have access to this treasure? Unlikely! There must be a relation of trust and sincere friendship, which is not always easy to establish and also takes years.

You have probably noticed that I never use the word "training", because it would be wrong in the internal martial arts — see the chapter on "Transmission". We train to run, to do a sport. We do it under the supervision of a trainer. The practice of an internal martial art is most often solitary, from time to time with a partner and periodically under the guidance of your teacher. The goal is to become your own Master one day. **This is self-evident, because the sensitive perception can only be of intimate nature.**

And to keep it simple, in the positive sense, our own practice should be compared to that of other traditions. There are Masters in the martial arts, but there are also Master Carpenters, bakers, chefs. Their background includes know-how, initiations, and also ethics. Theirs is a very tight-knit brotherhood, discreet, and teaches that the artwork[1] comes before the financial aspect. But is this always the case in the martial arts? Have we properly what has been bequeathed to us? I will let you find your own answer.

---

1. Artwork should be understood as what is being undertaken, but also one's own self.

The stages of learning

Ranking examinations should be ignored as they are often a way for federations or schools to control their members. The examinations are based on references that, because of the desire for official recognition, can only be very rational and therefore formal, which makes them very distant from the originating Tradition.

This first assertion can only shock, but the person in the best position to know your evolution is certainly your teacher — or yourself, above a certain level — unless he is... applying what the Chinese tradition mentions, "if you give kung fu to a student, you lose it!"

We must not forget that the notion of ranking is contemporary, preceded by the Menkyo in Japan, which validated a certain level of initiation, but not necessarily of acquisition — it is not enough to know something to be able to apply it — and that, in other Asian countries, the level of demonstrable kung fu — gong fu, accomplishment in an art — was the only guarantee of the level achieved.

Henceforth, rather than entertaining a controversy about the notion of "rewards" relative to the "official" grade, so characteristic of the modern man who needs to classify everything, the focus will be on the notion of progression.

To address an issue it is often necessary to draw a parallel with another field, on the condition to have a good knowledge of it. Yi quan can be used as an example here. It has been said in this school that "the technique does not exist", which has been taken at face value for a long time, maybe even today, if we look at the vague techniques that do not correspond to the precise usage of the body in this art. However, this principle is only true once the art has been mastered and cannot be applied by the disciple when still an apprentice or a companion, as the art is not yet "natural".

To understand this assertion, it is necessary to address the different stages of any form of apprenticeship — according to the progression described by the psychologist Abraham Maslow.

1. The learning progression in martial arts

A. Unconscious incompetence

That is to say, **"I do not know that I do not know."** Simply put, I do the techniques either in whatever manner or limited at the level of the principles used.

And, an important point, I am pleased with that.

So, logically, not only am I not seeking to learn new principles and not questioning what I do, but I also think that "everything is fine".

Even more surprising, I do not notice the body principles that some "old and tired" experts are using and that allow them to be more effective than many "young" practitioners, and I am not even aware of their existence.

I think that time will do its work without me questioning my achievements.

That is why it is said that "it is necessary to empty your cup to begin learning". Which is true on any level, once you encounter a Master worthy of the name.

B. Conscious incompetence

A very important stage: "**I know that I do not know**."

I am aware that what I do is imperfect and that I have "everything" to learn. **At this stage the learning can begin, or continue.**

I am not repeating a demonstrated technique with my previous knowledge, I try to understand a new way of functioning by "zeroing out" my fundamentals.

This is a very uncomfortable situation, because the feeling of losing all knowledge is now present. I become "clumsy" and "powerless", like a newborn learning to walk.

I will digress briefly here.

Training workshops are very fashionable nowadays. They consist, during a training session, in switching from the workshop of one school to that of another, while we have been taught in a third one.

We can take as an example a switch from shotokan karate to wa-doryu, then taiji and finally "contact" — *there are of course many more examples*.

The problem here is that the body principles in each school are different, as well as the overall approach. In the first two workshops in our example, we will see an opposite use of the hips and two different "philosophies"; in simple terms, one is direct and forceful, the other flexible and evading. The next workshop will show a search for the wholeness of the body, which requires a very different timing of the body segments — as well as a specific "internal" work. Lastly, "contact" teaches the use of gloves and body principles that do not correspond to any of the previous workshops. There is no coherence then, the practice becomes chaotic or else a personal *"melting pot"* of little interest in the long run — but the trainees can "get drunk" on multiple techniques.

The contemporary desire to learn a lot of techniques hampers not only any "internal" evolution, but also that in any art.

> *In that regard, the old Masters were known for the quality of a single technique of theirs. For example, Laoshi Guo Yun Shen of whom it was said that "Under all of Heaven, nothing may prevail against his Peng Chuan", reality and metaphor for the fact that every technique contains the entirety of the practice; we are coming back to "the technique does not exist" and paradoxically to the words of O'Sensei Ueshiba, "everything I do is technique".*

At the origin of many martial arts, the number of techniques was limited. The history of xing yi quan indicates that there were only "three authentic fists" — laosanquan. It was the same for *bagua zhang* — the *"three authentic palms"*, laosanzhang. Meanwhile, what is often forgotten, is that these three techniques can be "naturally" broken down into an infinite number of possibilities; if one understands their essence, of course.

In short, quantity of techniques and quality of teaching do not always go hand in hand.

C. Conscious competence

To arrive at this next stage, it appears necessary to remain in a permanently harmonious work, using the principles of a single teaching.

After a very long work, under the guidance of a good teacher obviously, the principles are finally understood and can be used. Only, they require strong concentration and attention. In one word, **they** are still "artificial": "I know, but it demands me an effort of concentration and attention."

This means that applying those principles can only be done in predefined situations, with a partner who also follows the pre-established rules.

That is why certain martial arts tirelessly repeat specific techniques and, when there is a "free" confrontation, their application becomes completely different, even opposite. To such a degree that practitioners are trained differently for "technique" and for "combat", even if it is conventional "combat".

It is not surprising that confusion in learning can occur if the rationales behind the principles are contradictory.

D. Lastly: unconscious competence

After **a coherent work** with the principles for a number of years, those become totally integrated in the receiver. They do not require any effort to be applied, **they are "natural" and are part of the spontaneous action of the practitioner**.

However, in the authentic arts, each stage can only be completed if it has become "natural".Then, everything must be repeated, as new principles are added "layer by layer" and require everything to be rethought.

So, every action becomes technique and is "proper" no matter the situation; that is to say, it corresponds to the precise synergy of the body segments that offers optimized dynamics.

In our field of interest this also means that the "internal" function developed also becomes "natural".

It can be said that the "essence" of the art is reached thanks to the "method" used and that, accordingly, it is possible to "leave the form". It has become natural to do "any type of action" in a "proper" way. **The form has been transcended, everything is "proper action".**

Through that experience, it can be seen how O'Sensei Ueshiba's words "everything I do is technique" agree with "the technique does not exist!".

History says that O'Sensei had trouble repeating his movements when the students asked him to. This is why an "old" Master is not always the best person to teach beginners.

That is the culmination of the method — but not the end of the practice.

> *You have noticed that I talk about principles and not techniques. That is to say, body principles — and theoretically, the associated internal connections — which include the timing of the body segments in the movement, as well as in shifting positions — and of course everything linked to the positioning relative to the adversary.*

In the end, it is important to note that the "technical form" kept as dogma in the practice, can become a straight jacket over time. As the metaphor goes: **"A tutor, who is useful in the beginning to help the tree grow, later becomes, if not taken away, the restraint that will make it a bonsai."** The allegory of the boat that has to be abandoned once the shore has been reached also applies.

Careful though, abandoning the boat too early is not a good idea either, as it may mark the end of the crossing...

These stages may have appeared obvious to some.

For the others, who doubt because of a lack of experience in their practice, we can take as an example an activity almost everyone is familiar with: driving.

- Let us skip the first stage: those who drive badly while thinking they are good drivers explain the number of accidents on the road each year.

- The second stage is when some people decide to improve their driving skills by questioning their abilities or who want to learn, knowing that they do not know how to drive.

- The third stage is learning, very technical, hands at "9 and 3 o'clock", paying attention, staying concentrated, movements according to a learned and repeated chronology, signs observed carefully and interpreted through a conscious analysis, same as the road. The route is defined by the teacher and is followed under his guidance. The whole thing is messy, clumsy and slow. Later, after obtaining the driving license, the young driver is still an apprentice like the occasional "Sunday driver".

- The fourth stage is achieved after several hundred thousand kilometers, when everything becomes easy, natural. The hands and feet act quickly and without conscious effort, at the right time, the signs are recognized and the road is a peaceful flow. The only potential problem, same as in the martial arts, is to underestimate the adversary, to trivialize, but that is another story...

We have now analyzed the stages of learning progression in the martial arts or in any other discipline. One can be a Master chef, or a Master in the martial arts. Of course, it is obvious that the stages are not always so easy to define precisely, which also explains some of the confusion encountered.

But where things get complicated is in the "internal" work, at least the one discussed in this book.

2. The progression in the internal martial arts

First and foremost, we should consider humans and their abilities. A key point:

Humans cannot do two things at the same time in a "reflective way" or "in awareness", with "sustained attention" — not to be confused with doing two things at the same time; the prerogative of women, it is said, who are required to constantly switch from one thing to another.

This notion needs further elaboration:

Of course, a good practice requires doing different movements with each arm, linked to each other, in relation to the spine, hips and legs, everything synchronized — according to the level of kung fu or accomplishment.

But, in contrast, humans cannot write two different texts, one with the right hand, another with the left, even those who are ambidextrous. Same as it is not possible to reflect on two subjects at the same time. On a sensitive level, if you are suffering enormously from a tooth ache you cannot discern the taste differences between two dishes; if you are particularly moved by a vision, you forget its surroundings. The list goes on indefinitely.

This particularity, characteristic of humans, is often forgotten in the learning of internal arts.

It can be concluded that the stages defined previously cannot and should not be respected.

More specifically:

- **If you are learning a specific technique that requires your full attention, you cannot at the same time use your intention**—your Yi—**correctly,** since the latter, as long as it does not exist naturally, also requires your attention/concentration—except when the Yi is natural, after more than ten years of "proper" practice.

An often forgotten fact...

- That is why, to develop the "quality" of your Yi and to put in all of your "intention/attention/ concentration", it is necessary to do simple techniques for a number of years—zhan zhuang is a perfect example for this.

- Thus, on a daily basis, while performing "slow" techniques—for example, "shili", "testing the force" in yi quan, the forms in taiji, or the ame no tori fune undo, "rowing movement " in aikido—it is important to take a few minutes to correct your form and then work with your intention— *Yi*—for many minutes.

To facilitate the understanding of the stages of progression in the internal arts, let us return to the previous chronology:

A. Unconscious incompetence

Meaning, "**I do not know that I do not know**".

Obvious, because without question there is no answer.

B. Conscious incompetence

A very important stage: "**I know that I do not know.**"

Here too, I am aware that what I do is imperfect and that I have "everything" to learn.

These are the "basics of the basics" of all learning.

In the internal dimension it must be accepted that "**one's own perception is today limited but can be extended toward new unknown horizons**".

It is this last point that is important, to admit that "**one cannot apprehend the future development of one's own perception and, most importantly, to not want to control it through the intellect**".

As will be emphasized later on, the cultural input, as attractive as it may be, can become an obstacle on the path. In particular, if it serves as a filter of one's own progression. Taoism, like Buddhism, has been a victim of the Chinese scholars who have tempted to explain the unexplainable; but, as it is known in these arts, "The realm of experience escapes any analysis"; I will come back to that in another chapter.

Note that this last point is in total contradiction with current education, which is based on the idea that "each element must be addressed by the intellect upstream".

Accordingly, the practitioner must then make a real effort to remain in the sense realm. **As with all esoteric initiations, the discourse analysis, and therefore logic, must only be applied downstream, after the experimented sense realm and not the other way around. This is undoubtedly the reason for the secrecy surrounding them. If one is not willing to accept this principle, it seems pointless to follow this kind of path**.

When it comes to learning techniques, you must, as I mentioned already, limit yourself to a very small number and forget "any" willingness to apply them.

Moreover, some time ago, the Tradition was saying: before any practice, it is necessary to do, for three years, a *proper* "standing meditation"[1] for one to three hours a day.

A little aside concerning taiji quan — *tai chi chuan*: the combination of 108 movements — or less for the short form — must be performed without the need to recall them; this is, for a long time, the only possible way to be in a "permanent" Yi. A classic yet surprising method, and which is but a preparatory step for an involved practice, is to be able to act — by feeling the movements — while watching TV. The "long-term memory" can thus be activated. Additionally, this attention toward "something else" will prepare the practitioner to later carry this same attention toward the Yi.

It is important to note that one day the form must be abandoned and everything must become "natural", something that is often forgotten...

I remember telling my Chinese teachers that after learning the

---

1. See chapter "Standing meditation".

techniques of five different styles of karate, of thai boxing and of close combat, for 25 years, I did not "only" want to learn new ones, but rather "to know what hides behind them". It is only after this clarification that I was considered.

C. Conscious competence

This stage, in the prescribed work, corresponds to the presence of the "substance" — Qi — inside oneself. The practitioner feels inside him a dense "matter", which invades the body when in zhan zhuang or when using the Yi. Something that requires attention and concentration.

As a reminder, this "matter" or "substance" is what is also called "breath" or "Qi" (Chi), "Ki". But in a practice that is not supposed to be abstract, it is desirable to bring this notion back to a concrete sensitive perception, that of a "substance which evolves with time".

This "presence" begins in the hands, then moves progressively to the arms, then the body and finally the legs.

Each zhang zhuang has as its objective to involve certain specific parts of the body. At this stage, the practitioner can learn new techniques. They will allow him to move using the body principles, which offer the possibility to consciously activate the presence of the "substance" and the possibility to "knead" it, a bit like dough. The practice must always be split in a short time for auto-correction of the technique followed by long minutes of work with the Yi.

D. The last stage: unconscious competence

After a long work consisting of one to three hours per day of "standing meditation" and one hour of "slow techniques" — long form taiji or shili — at the end of seven to ten years, the practitioner can hope for an awakening of the Yi. It is natural and permanently active at every moment, it is "substance".

The substance is then in a "gaseous" state. So, the permeability of the body exists — see next — "the door is open".

It is at this stage that the practitioner can act freely.

The technique is supported by the "substance" — same as is the body — and does not require any physical effort. The body is one, every technique, every action is one — wholeness of the body. The "lack of opening" in all actions — silk thread maintained in the movement and "between movements" — is "natural" since the "substance" is present. The ability to apply — the force — is also "substance".

It is necessary to verify this ability on a partner who is not "complicit" (voluntarily or involuntarily). Otherwise, the practitioner remains in a comfortable illusion of perception whose creator is the unconscious — said ability must be superior to what the body can produce physically when used in an "ordinary" way.

The practitioner has been able to verify the application of the "substance" by respecting the following progression:

1. In the beginning, without moving, in a "standing meditation" — zhan zhuang;

2. Next, by slowly moving in place — form or shili;

3. Slow steps — bu;

4. With a partner, slowly — tuishou;

5. With speed — fali, fajing;

6. Finally, naturally — kong jin.

This last step of "kong jin" — empty force — is where everything is natural. But it is far removed from any demonstrative aspect. In fact, everything becomes understated, without extravagance, without useless outbursts, without expressive Jingshen. Only a trained eye can recognize this state.

But does the practitioner really want that?

Our mental functioning

We saw in detail the basics of understanding internal martial arts, the principles, the mistakes to avoid, the important things not to miss. After that, we analyzed the different stages of learning. The picture will not be complete though, without taking into account our own mental functioning, that of our brain.

The accepted model of functioning is, for most martial arts experts, the one defined by Dr. Paul Donald MacLean under the name "triune brain".

To begin with, it would be senseless not to advise reading the theory of this neurobiologist and, in particular, the three basic texts, *The Triune Brain,* as well as the works of another neurobiologist, Dr. Henri Laborit. And lastly, to complete the list, the works of Master Henri Plée.

In the meantime though, here is what you will find next:

- A synthesis of what I deem to be necessary knowledge for a practitioner;
- And a short explanation of how that theory applies to the martial side of the practice.

1. Synthesis of the theory of the triune brain[1]

Today, the hypothesis of the evolution of the human brain in three separate stages is being disputed. However, the description of the functional organization itself appears particularly correct in terms of behavior. In fact, the principles of the theory are used in many and various fields: management education, marketing, personal development and, essential to us, martial arts.

These three brains would have appeared progressively during the evolution of our species: reptile, passing through mammalian, to ar-

1. Synthesis based on : Paul D. MacLean, *The Triune Brain in Evolution: Role in Paleocerebral Functions.*

rive at *"Homo Sapient"* that we are supposed to be — *Homo sapiens* or "wise man" in Latin.

The three brains are superimposed: the reptilian — cerebral trunk — the mammalian — paleomammalian, limbic system — the neocortex — neomammalian, intellect.

Their respective functions are as follows:

- The reptilian is the "primitive" brain, found in reptiles, birds, fish. Its main function is survival. It is responsible for homeostasis, that is to say, "the dynamic balance" of our bodies, by regulating the heart, breathing, temperature etc., in one word the vital functions. In the latter, one should not forget drinking, eating and finally reproducing (primary for any species, whether animal or vegetal);

- The mammalian or limbic system, called by Dr. Paul D. MacLean "the visceral brain of survival", appeared with the first mammalians. Its function is to be the "physiological centre of emotions". For Dr. H. Laborit it is the seat of affection, of the ritual — social integration, the group — of convictions, beliefs, motivation, feeling of security, and most importantly, of long-term memory;

- The neocortex is most developed in humans. It is the "intellectual" brain, allowing logical reasoning, language, anticipation. H. Laborit adds that it can also create new structures, "the imaginary structures".

It also allows the "recognition of an object as an external reality in a given space".[1]

It is easy to see why being preoccupied with one's appearance during practice only concerns the superficial aspect of humans.

The main thing to remember is still to follow.

The neocortex gives us awareness of our existence, the famous "Cogito, ergo sum" — I think, therefore I am. This means that the conscious "Self" is limited to this brain, although, as H. Laborit states, "it can only think and suggest. It does not know and cannot do anything" and adds: "The brain does not do anything, its supposed intelligent part is subjected and the primitive part decides

---

1. Henri Laborit, Éloge de la fuite, Éditions Gallimard.

without its opinion."[1] Which means that our will cannot control the other two brains.

We find here, again, the fundamental idea that learning martial arts cannot be done through reasoned action.

In short, our neocortex depends on the limbic system, which itself depends on the reptilian brain. The usual explanatory image is that of a ship: the captain is the reptilian brain, the second in command is the limbic system, the passenger is the neocortex, or the "Self"...

We can see why all Traditions, initiatory, esoteric and, in our case, martial, have as their purpose an action on the deep brain structures — for example, the allegory of Theseus and the Minotaur. Since the neocortex cannot have any influence on the other two brains, these Traditions use means that touch on the sense realm, to wit: emotional shock, all kinds of abstinence, exhaustion, suffering, reiteration. It is this fundamental point that seems to have been forgotten today in the majority of various practices.

2. Applying the theory to the martial arts

The most important thing to remember, to my mind, concerns the neocortex, or to put it differently: the reason, the intellect, the analysis, the discourse, the speculation, the will. In one word, "oneself", or at least the awareness that you have around your "Self".

The neocortex then cannot decide an action, unless the mammalian and reptilian brains allow it. However, in that case, every voluntary action will be slow and clumsy. The example with driving fits here too; so long as it is at the level of voluntary attention, it will be clumsy.

On the other hand, the reptilian brain can decide, and the mammalian and the neocortex cannot do anything about it. In the same way, the mammalian brain can also make you act without your knowledge. This is why the theory states that 95% to 98% of our actions are guided by the deep brains without us being aware of it.

All of the above is therefore very important for any approach concerning our mental functioning. And if we apply MacLean's theory to the martial arts, it will look like this:

---

1. Alain Resnais, *My American Uncle*, film based on the work of H. Laborit.

- A martial art learned through reasoning is at the level of the short-term memory, the neocortex. The result of such an education is slow and clumsy. It can only be applied in a situation free of any stress. Actually, the lack of stress is "the" reason why the other two brains "let go";

- A martial art taught through repetition and instinct—**reflex**—in a method of codified combat, that is to say ritualist, is at the level of the ritual—**dominant male**—so, at the level of the long-term memory and the mammalian brain. Speed of action and reaction are three times faster compared to the neocortex.

Fights inside a training club, competitions, and even challenges are at this level. Even brawls, unless... one of the adversaries switches to the reptilian wanting to eliminate the other or others.

However, in the case of survival—**when the reptilian decides that its life is in danger**—what is left from what we have managed to learn? The answer is "nothing from the theoretical learning", because it is the reptilian brain that acts. This is the natural instinctive dynamic, with a speed of action or reaction 30 times faster compared to the neocortex. The reptilian will choose between two options: flee or kill the other, and occasionally inhibition: physical and mental block. Exceptionally, it can also trigger an "act of madness", like running after someone armed with a gun.

So, how would martial arts teaching function in this last case? Three solutions appear possible:

- The first one: "going into survival mode", meaning:
  - Working the animal vitality, so it can appear the moment it is needed— **"Jingshen", the number one element of martial effectiveness. Note that the "direction" of Jingshen can be multiple; from martial (even purely animal) to spiritual, depending on the person,**
  - Reconditioning the body for an optimal "natural" functioning—**to have "kung fu", martial accomplishment of the body, in second place in the order of martial importance;**

- The second solution: to receive a "brainwashing" for the consecutive reaction, or to put it otherwise:
  - Visualization work—**or a simulation**—of an extreme situation

with emotion, exhaustion, suffering and a simple action — i.e. act to kill, for example: military training — but which does not always work or works too well — overreaction to the risk; who would want to become a dangerous animal?

- Without forgetting that in survival mode, there is often a "black out" — people forget what they are doing and only a few images survive as a "memory";

- Lastly, the third solution and the less obvious one: not going into survival mode and applying everything learned on the level of the long-term memory of the mammalian brain — the technique, in third place in the order of importance in martial arts; but it must be remembered that the "self" does not decide. The only possibility is that this type of situation happens often...

During the battle of Stalingrad it was observed that the "fresh" Russian troops, those without experience, were more effective than the combat-seasoned German ones. Why? Because the few survivors amongst those arriving were in a state of survival madness, thus horribly effective. The Germans, on the other hand, in survival mode for much longer, were "trivializing" the risks in their minds.

The metaphor mentioned earlier, of a man who crosses a wooden beam, is the typical illustration of the interaction between the three brains:

- At 30 centimeters above the ground, without any risk; demonstration or competition, controlled confrontation: mammalian brain;

- At 2 meters, if I fall, I will hurt myself; fight with KOs: mammalian brain;

- At 5 meters, "non-conventional" fight, without weapons; if I fall, I could really hurt myself: mammalian or reptilian brain, depending on the person;

- At 10 meters, if I fall, I risk my life: reptilian brain — or, exceptionally, mammalian if the act is trivialized.

However, it can all vary depending on the individual: if, at 30 centimeters above the ground, you are in survival mode, then you are sick and dangerous...

What about the internal martial arts then? We can see how internal work, with its objective of influencing the deep brains, can really transform the practitioner. However, depending on the direction given, the repercussions can be very different, something we will address later on. On this topic, there is the edifying example of O'Sensei Ueshiba who managed to transform the art of war of his teacher Sogaku Takeda into an art of spiritual dimension. There is every reason to think that the influence of Onisaburo Deguchi of the Omoto sect—Shinto-inspired—was a determinant in his choices. A metamorphosis that I have also seen in a Chinese Master who frequented Taoist and Buddhist monks.

It can be concluded that the effect of the ambient environment is, without doubt, in the practice of internal arts, a factor in the practitioner's evolution.

3. The different types of rituals according to Konrad Lorenz

The interest in knowing the various types of rituals is not about having a critical eye on those with whom we interact, but rather to *observe* oneself in a way to *gain some perspective* relative to one's own actions and reactions. The goal is, as with any personal development, to step out of our animal nature.

Let us begin with what the biologist Konrad Lorenz stated: "The instinctive behavior of animals, humans included, is determined by innate stimuli, not learned ones", which he called the "innate mechanisms triggering behavior".[1] These rituals of the limbic realm, or otherwise the unconscious, practically identical to those of the big apes, dictate instinctive actions and reactions. Only the fear of punishment and rejection by the group, also part of the limbic system, can stop them.

What are these rituals and what do they consist of? Concerning our subject, these are:[2]

- The ritual of territory: vital for the animal, to feed, to protect the female—for the male, to protect the offspring—for the female. In humans this translates into the unintentional and

1. Developed from: Konrad Lorenz, *Evolution and Modification of Behavior*.
2. Henry Plée, *The sublime and ultimate art of vital points*.

improper reactions of the driver (vehicle = territory), the tribal rites of fans, the belonging to a martial arts school.

- The ritual of seduction: the peacock shows its tail, the young man his muscles or his nice car. The young woman wears a tight pair of jeans, shows her cleavage. The martial arts practitioner displays his beautiful technique in front of an audience of both sexes;
- The ritual of submission — the young wolf rolls on its back to show its defenseless vital organs, the student submits to the technique of the Master or the teacher;
- The ritual of domination — the lion roars and the young males run away, the soldier shows his medals, the practitioner his diplomas, his belt and dan;
- The ritual of provocation — the gorilla beats its chest, the rugby team does its hakka, the competitor stares down the adversary and shouts a loud — pseudo — Kiai.
- The ritual of confrontation — deers wrestle during the rut, the young men fight on the dance floor, the practitioners confront each other in codified encounters, the elderly during theoretical debates.

There are of course many other examples.

4. One possible approach to the "spiritual"

For those who are searching, thanks to the practice of an internal art, some form of spiritual fulfillment, there is something specific to remember. I will remind it: the neocortex allows "the recognition of an object as an external reality in a given space". This means that it — the reason, the intellect, the analysis, the discourse, the speculation, the will — separates us from a certain external reality on a perceptual level. It thus creates our "bubble of individuality", which is "only" broken by our five senses.

That is why, same as previously, an intellectual approach cannot achieve a modification of your perception. Text analyses, whatever they might be, religious or esoteric, can "only" be indicators — same as this guide strives to be. Any speculation is thus limited. Only the actual practice — in the sense of body/mind — together with the tools of the Tradition, can potentially offer a real and concrete "broadening of the field of consciousness", and this, because the latter have been created to have an effect on the deep brains. As we will see together later on, the "breath" is the link that allows this broadening.

However, it also has to be conform to the practitioner's own nature!

The breath: Qi, Ki

Ah! This trendy mystery, the Qi — or Ki in Japanese! A mystery that makes dream every person eager to find an inner dimension allowing to escape one's own limits. Exotic in the West, where simple and pleasant methods are offered for its development, as much for health or spiritual reasons as for martial ones. An equally mysterious element in Asia, where "Masters" act at a distance on unfortunate volunteers with this magical fluid. Which contemporary books take up in their theories, digging in Taoist scriptures and Chinese medicine... Mystery of mysteries, abstraction, magical fluid. The list could easily go on. Exaggeration? A bit, only a little bit...

Most fighters realistic about martial arts, or combat sports, smile kindly but laugh inside when they hear this word. And even adherents of internal arts, at least those of an authentic tradition, can understand why. I remember my old Master who said vituperatively: "Nonsense!", when seeing the Qi peddlers in Beijing's parks. Of course, as in any field, there are serious people, but often, in contrast, displaying services for commercial ends is not always a proof of authenticity. Smoke and mirrors to attract the customer.

So, to avoid the abstraction allowing to affirm everything of a notion that is, for most people, immaterial and therefore irrefutable, we will address this subject through experience.

To begin with, an introduction. Same as the refusal of any concrete aspect of the Qi hinders its perception, defining it intellectually creates a difficult to overcome psychological barrier.

To paraphrase the Prayer of the Cats Abbey, who said: "To define God is to distance oneself from Him!"; while we can say "To define the Qi is to distance oneself from it!". Indeed, this is how the authentic traditions see it.

Moreover, it is important not to oppose education and tools used, as some practitioners, coming from a professional scientific background, tend to do. We are not in the realm of discourse analysis, but in that of experience. **One must accept the possibility of the existence of the "breath" and wait for a result that the imagination cannot, and should not, define.**

A reminder: the "Qi" in Chinese, or "Ki" in Japanese, is a principle that can be translated, according to Taoist alchemy, as "breath". We should avoid the usual translation as "energy". Indeed, it appears too virtual, even though the term "sells" better today.

The following *note* by Catherine Despeux seems quite accurate:

> *"Customarily, internal Qi is translated as "energy", more particularly in medical texts. We prefer to use the word "breath", because the external Qi or external breath is not different in nature from the internal Qi or internal breath. Furthermore, in texts on internal alchemy, the movement of the internal breath is understood as being similar to that of respiration, with an inspiration and an expiration."*[1]

Concretely: the internal work experience allows to, progressively "in the long term", feel the Qi as a kind of "matter" inside the body. Matter that I would call "**substance**", **because this is how it is perceived on the sensitive level. This "substance", over the years of practice, transforms in fluidity to one day exit and enter the body in awareness. The acquired "permeability" of the body to the Qi feels as if one "inspires and expires" through all the pores of the body, similar to breathing**—a notable difference is that, after more than twenty years of regular practice, "inspiration and expiration" occur simultaneously, a paradox that only experience can explain.

> *The concrete aspect of the breath, hence the term "substance", avoids the creation of subjective feelings such as "I feel the energy in me", "I feel a ball of energy in my hands", "I feel the energy of some thing". It is desirable to pass through concrete steps. To test what is believed to be a result with people who are not part of the same school. This, in order to avoid many disillusions. Here I am reminded of an anecdote. A friend, enthusiastic about exotic energy arts, asked me to try a Qi emitter he had bought in China. The thing was made of a parabolic part on top of a support, in which was inserted a tube filled with a mysterious liquid. "The effect is surprising!" he said, because while at a taiji workshop all the participants had been impressed by*

1. *Traité d'Alchimie et de physiologie taoiste*, translation of Zhao Bichen's Treatise of Alchemy and Taoist Medicine by Catherine Despeux.

the strength of the Qi emission of the machine. Moreover, three women had lost consciousness under its action.

So, curious, we positioned ourselves, a few students and me, in front of the machine. Ten minutes passed, then fifteen, during which we were looking at each other interrogatively. After half an hour we became bored and I had the harsh task of destroying an illusion.

It is without doubt due to the similarity of the perception to physiological breathing that the term "breath" has been universally retained. We can find this notion in traditions other than Far- eastern ones. To quote but a few: *Prana* in Sanskrit, *Pneuma* in Greek, *Ruach* in Hebrew, *Ruh* in Arabic, *Spiritus* in Latin. Saint Paul differentiated between "pneumatikos" and "psychikos" — respectively, people at the spiritual level and those who have not yet attained it. Gnostic Christians have taken up this opposition by differentiating the "hylics", matter-bound, "psychics", Christians cut off from the truth, and "pneumatics", who have the "Knowledge", who have attained the Gnosis.[1]

But we are getting out of topic (although...).

An important thing to note is that the Latin *"spiritus"*, meaning "spirit", does not evoke the same image to the Western collective unconscious, hence the loss, most probably, of many reference points.

The advantage of this "ecumenical viewpoint" is that it avoids us to err into an undesirable exoticism. **Man is man, whatever his origin, color, nationality, religion. Consequently, the actual essence of man is universal, as well as the essence of the original traditions bequeathed to him. Only the cultural veneer is different. Unfortunately, very often, too often, the "specialists" study the "packaging differences" rather than search for this common essence.**

However, this translation, "breath", can bring about some serious confusion. The most common one is to associate the notion uniquely with physiological breathing. But, as I will explain later, **the "breath", the Qi, is a "substance that surrounds everything and permeates everything",** and this is not some theory, but the actual perception of the practitioner.

1. *Le Souffle — Sous le sceau du secret*, Le Mercure Dauphinois, p.31 (from the same author).

What Man is missing is the perception of this "substance" inside him—and outside. So, he cannot vary his relation to it. **He must regain the sense that allows him to densify it inside himself, then to "knead" it, to make it fluid, to finally increase the "permeability" of his body in order to consciously commune.** Of course, this relation exists by the nature of every thing. However, the communion with the "substance" can only be very weak, since it is **"asleep", without awareness**—see next chapter.

This can be compared to ambient music that one ends up not hearing, too preoccupied by reflective thoughts.

Going back to the confusion about breathing. The "Asanas" in yoga are a *tool* that has the function to perceive and later density the *Prana*. Exactly like the zhan zhuang—*ritsu zen*—in the internal martial arts. The "Pranayama" is a tool using the respiration to guide the *Prana* inside oneself, same as all the "slow forms linked to the Yi" in the internal arts.

However, as in any Tradition, one must be initiated to have the "know-how". *Breathing for the sake of breathing* cannot work—a very common mistake, same as technique for the sake of technique. **Just as in the martial arts, breathing without using the perceived "substance" can be good for health, but useless to guide the Qi. Which is also true for body movement.** This is what I will try to show you in this book. The respiration can be a tool to work on the "breath". Just as sound and body movement can be—and one day thought; for example, the authentic prayer.

But most importantly, confusion of all confusions, it is essential **to not confound the tool with the objective.** And thus, **to not amalgamate the means with the objective**.

A few examples of this mistake:

- Doing yoga postures for the sake of performance, without knowledge of the internal work;
- Doing demonstrative Pranayama, but not guiding the Prana;
- Doing a zhan zhuang physically, but without awakening an awareness of the "substance";
- Doing breath work, but without guiding the "substance"—be-

cause there has not been an awakening of awareness of this substance;

- Doing slow and gracious, or dense, movements, using isometrics and the tendinous structures, but without guiding the "substance".

That is to say, remaining in the image of the self, or in the practical aspect of the tool, while forgetting the objective. From this confusion follow many illusions in the martial arts, for example:

- Kokyu, which is only a breathing exercise, with the "hara" as a theoretical principle;
- Kiai — uniting the breath — which is only a piercing scream — while it can be inaudible;
- Shi sheng — testing the sound — which is only a vocal exercise — while it can be inaudible;
- Kotodama — sacred words — of which some magical repercussions are expected;
- Fajing, which are only fali — done uniquely through physical strength;
- "Expressions of wholeness", which are only mimicked actions;
- "Principles of the silk thread, of rooting", which are but physical pursuits.
- Etc.

All of the tools mentioned are of great quality, but if the "breath" is not present and is not perceived by the practitioner, they lose all "substance".

The Chinese tradition often divides the Qi in several notions. To name a few, among others:

- Yuan Qi: original breath,
- Zheng Qi: sum of innate and acquired breaths,
- Zong Qi: ancestral breath,
- Jing Qi: essential or seminal breath,
- Ying Qi: nourishing breath,
- Wei Qi: defensive breath.

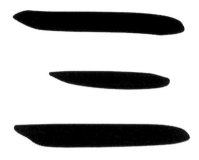

The primitive character for Oi

Note that, for the practitioner, this differentiation corning from Chinese medicine can improve general knowledge, but it will not be useful to advance in the practice of internal arts. As is often the case, the confusion is between "knowing" and "experiencing". What is essential to remember is that: **"Although there are many types of Qi, all of them are one Qi".** And, on a practical level, the will to differentiate is but an additional obstacle.

Certain metaphors are also worthy of interest, like this one from Zhao Bichen:

"What is the Qi? Qibo answers: the upper burner opens and spreads the scents of five cereals which penetrate the muscles, fill the body and irrigate the hairs, like mist or humid dew; this is what is called the Qi.1"

Very beautiful, is it not?

Let us remain pragmatic though and avoid creating, as in modern Qi Gong, dreams that will only serve as support for subjective perceptions. In internal work, the progression must be verifiable. The Qi, the "substance", must be perceived in a tangible way, especially because it will have to be used against a partner or even an opponent. What has been bequeathed to us is a tool to improve the physical possibilities in the case of a confrontation. Not long ago, it was not about role playing, but a question of survival. Hence, any illusion could have only been rejected by the "ancients". In contrast, today, the internal dimension of martial arts is most often directed at individual self-realization. Nonetheless, this does not reduce the effective-

1. Traité d'Alchimie..., op.cit.

ness of the tools; but the ancestral "know-how" must be respected.

The progression of the perception of the Qi is more or less long, depending on the time allocated to the tools every day. In general, it takes three to five years, at one to three hours per day, to begin feeling the "substance" inside the whole body. This perception, as I will explain later in the "standing meditation", begins in the hands, then moves progressively to the arms, then the body and finally the legs.

The practitioner has then the feeling of being transformed into a "tubby Michelin man", meaning "inflated", pneumatic — look! Same as the Greek expression or that of Saint Paul. This feeling is present during practice, then disappears after it, and one day becomes permanent. The density of the breath will increase with time, as will the kung fu.

The practitioner will then have the feeling of being carried by his own breath. The "here and now" will be presence of the "substance"and consequently, the natural Yi will allow to not have an "opening", the "silk thread" will be maintained. The tools, which we are going to discuss later, will allow to *"knead"* this "substance" in order to make it more malleable. After that, if the practitioner possesses the necessary qualities, it can become more fluid. And one day maybe gaseous, able to enter and exit the body as a respiration. It is at this level that one's physical abilities can be transcended. Every movement will be felt like a respiration through all skin pores.

Then, with time and persistence, the "unified breathing", inspiration and expiration occurring at the same time, will allow the practitioner to use the universal Qi in his practice, more or less. Lastly, if "the door is opened to him", if "the Tao welcomes him" — his "bubble of individuality" will explode, **"his divided consciousness joining the undivided one".** This is not a theory, but experience. (Anyway, this is outside the subject of this book) We find here the four states of the Western and Buddhist Traditions: solid, liquid, gaseous, ethereal.

On a practical level:

- **The solid state of the "breath" makes one clumsy and is not really applicable;**
- **The liquid state is applicable, but limited;**

- **The gaseous state allows to surpass one's own limits**;
- **The ethereal state... Maybe one day, but that is another story**.

So, may the "breath" be in you!

Complementary notions

1. The Yi

It has happened to everyone to feel stared at. One turns around, looks in a specific direction and discovers who is the observer. One wonders how is that possible... And what is the origin of the perception of this stare. There are often multiple answers: unconscious, instinct, chance etc. And, another possibility, what if the phenomenon of our own perception was linked to the intention directed by the observer, which we exceptionally felt, that is to say, a form of supra-sensory *relation*?

For the experimented practitioner, or for the person training with an expert, the answer is obvious. In part, this is what is called "Yi" in Chinese. The Chinese medical glossaries state that the Yi is "the ideation, the thought, the idea, the memory that manifests through the formation of an idea and an intention in the heart". Which is, to say the least, confusing, and tends to amalgamate the reflective, the neocortex, with the unconscious, to wit "the intention of the heart".

Nevertheless, I will personally keep that last point in mind, which is somewhat reminiscent of the "Logos" — usually translated as: "word", "verb", but also and mainly as "reason of the heart that produces the intention" — and which allows, according to Plato, to exit the *cave* and therefore the limits of perception of the common man. A surprising parallel with the work in the internal arts, but do not forget that the Greeks were adept at contemplation, which can lead to the same result.

Back to the Yi. In my previous works, some fifteen years ago, I mentioned that for practical purposes this principle corresponds:

• To the intention, meaning an impulse that leads the action in a specific direction;

• To the attention, mental concentration allowing to send the entirety of one's interiority in that direction;

- The perceptual imagination, sensitive to the objective and to the journey to be accomplished.

These are the details of the work to be done, allowing the practitioner to lean on something concrete and go toward a sense realm that he is not yet aware of.

To approach this principle, some simple examples of Yi can be mentioned:

- The lumberjack swinging his axe toward the tree, his eyes/intention directed at the objective;
- The archer sending his arrow toward the target already reached;
- The judoka, the aikidoka, performing a throw in the direction of the intention given by their eyes.
- Etc.

Moreover, if we wish to improve our Yi, it appears necessary to use examples from *everyday life* where a "sensitive connection" exists, like:

- The praying person, directing a prayer toward the cross, a place, a Buddha;
- The father or mother, opening their arms to their child, whom they have not seen for a long time — the connection existing before the physical contact.

In those two examples, the "opening/intention of the heart" seems evident. However, despite these examples, which can indicate some certain way to approach the principle, there is obviously an essential element missing.

What is it? It is the relation between Yi and Qi — "substance" or "breath", according to the level achieved.

The Yi does not have only a nerve and motor control function, intended for the muscles, which would be a grave error of interpretation, but rather to move the Qi, with time and patience. **The "Yi" in the internal arts is the sense that allows to guide the Qi inside the body, but also from the interior to the exterior and inversely**. At least, that is how it might be one day.

Why this notion of "sense"? **Because we really are talking about the "sensitive reeducation" of a sense that is asleep.** It can be considered that humans have lost awareness of this "sense" and that the work to be done consists in awakening the practitioner's awareness to it. And this, so that one day the Yi becomes "natural" and no longer requires any perceptual effort. Same like sight, smell, hearing, touch, taste, do not require any effort to be used.

It must be emphasized that for this sensory function to exist, Yi and Qi must be linked and end up fusing. But, a rather important point, this "fusion" allows to guide the Qi **"through the Yi"**:

- In the movement — *performing arts, martial arts, yoga,*
- In the sound — *Kiai, Shi sheng, Mantra, Dhikr,*
- In the physiological inhalation and exhalation — *pranayama, kokyu,*
- And, for some, in the spiritual intention.

Everything becomes identical, "relation interior/exterior" in awareness. Furthermore, the "Yi/Qi' equally allows to receive a sensory perception, not only of the internal Qi, but also of that external. (Which is outside the scope of this guide).

To do that, the reeducation must follow progressively the precise transmission of the Tradition.

2. The Jingshen

The Chinese medicine abstracts indicate that:

> *"The Jingshen combines into one notion the aspect of Shen — the spirit — namely the spiritual, mental and emotional activities of man, and the notion of Jing — the prenatal and postnatal essence — meaning the mental and emotional systems through which the brain responds to stimuli from the external world. The spiritual abilities and emotional responses."*[1]

I will also add: "the response to stimuli from the internal world".

In this explanation, I think it is best to retain "responses to stimuli from the external world" — and internal — and "spiritual abilities and emotional responses". In sum, "stimuli, emotion and spirit". The internal arts tradition leans particularly on these elements in its work. *It is not enough* to work with the Yi — intention, new sense — the internal perception must also be amplified, as well as the external relation with "the object". The objective of this perceptual state is

---

1. V. Terrier, http://www.sinoptic.ch/qigong/

to be attentive to the smallest sensitive variation perceived. To do that, it is necessary to set "the potentiometer" of one's senses not to agitation, a common mistake, but, in a subtle way, to the objective that every change, every evolution is a conscious one.

The "Jingshen" corresponds to this phenomenon. It intensifies the "vitality of the mind", which in turn allows to heighten the sensory perception and, with time, the supra-sensory one — the Yi, the Qi, the Shen, and consequently, the spirit of decision and action. This is the number one quality that the practitioner of martial arts must have. The tradition is clear on this. **The qualities of the martial artist are in the following order of importance** (as previously seen):

1. Jingshen
2. Kung fu — accomplishment
3. Technical knowledge

A small precision, the "kung fu" — *gongfu in pinyin* — is the level of accomplishment that makes the body dense and activates it in its entirety, resulting in real effectiveness.

It should be noted that technical knowledge comes last in the list. Indeed, even "without technique", a person possessing the two previous qualities, *Jingshen and kung fu,* is still fearsome. The experience of every fighter confirms the importance of "Jingshen". If, in front of you, appears a man ready to do anything, ignited with what some call the "spirit of madness", two solutions become available — succeeding in getting on his level of vitality, or otherwise fleeing. Defeat is practically certain if you are unable to achieve a similar state.

In sport, "Jingshen" has been translated as "the eye of the tiger". The tradition indicates that this notion of internal vitality is seen in the gaze, the eyes — but it can also be added that this vitality is linked to the unconsciously perceived Yi. The intensity of the gaze shows a capacity for fearsome determination and an intense vitality.

A single nuance can be added: the "Jingshen" is not a kind of madness, but a different state offering the possibility to use the essential resources of man. Furthermore, this state will one day allow to *sublimate* the mind.

However, the direction given can vary between practitioners. Some experts teach and themselves work with images of de-

struction, exploding organs, internal hemorrhage, on imaginary adversaries. This is not very far from the notion of madness. It may have been a solution in the past, but today it is an obvious deviation.

This "spirit of vitality" can also be directed at the spiritual through an extension of one's "field of perception", which is essential in both internal work and esoteric quests. The examples abound. The representation of Guru Rinpoche, Padmasambhava, whose eyes present an evident "Jingshen", could be mentioned. Often mistakenly understood as an "angry look". The zen metaphor that "one should meditate as if there were a tiger standing in front" is of the same nature. We find here the spiritual capacities described previously.

The "Jingshen" is therefore essential in the work to be done. It must be used in zhan zhuang, in "slow movements guided by the Yi", in tuishou, and of course in fights and attacks, whether they are called "Jiji" or "Shiai". It is essential, in the case of a non-conventional confrontation, not to suffer the adversary. However, the desire to destroy the opponent, in my opinion, is not a good thing for one's own mental health. Laoshi Wang XJ takes an image allowing to avoid this pitfall: "You are escaping a fire. The opponent is the obstacle to your exit". No hate, no negative thoughts.

However, I would **put the bar even lower for everyday** practice. As an allegory, I will use a personal image: **"A bit like when you are trying to hear a murmur, waking up to hear not only the inaudible, but also something that your senses do not perceive anymore".** Note also that "Jingshen" is essential to emit the "breath" and to receive it. Of course, when the level is adequate, any variation of the "Jingshen" is possible, depending on the days, on the situations, on the instinct. But, in the meantime, how to be in the "proper state"? As always, no speculation, but a past experience must be used. Only it can provoke a response from your unconscious. Be concrete, no dreams, no "movies". Take an event that has left you with an exceptional sensory exaltation, for example:

- A sunrise or a sunset on a horizon that gave you the impression of pulling you in;
- A potentially risky situation you managed to escape thanks to an action lead by something that escapes you;

- An astonishment that did not "sweep you off your feet";
- An exceptional encounter that changed your life.

And for those who absolutely want something martial:

- You are encircled by enemies ready to attack you — but be careful, this image, if of a real experience, should not, like a sound too loud, make you "deaf".

Use that memory as a support, visualize it, feel it, then let the image drift away, but keep the sense of exaltation — without agitation, with an inner smile — and work with the appropriate tool. With time this state is linked to the Yi when the latter is "natural". Lastly, it must be repeated, without "Jingshen" there is no progress!

3. Receptors and emitters of Qi

It is conceivable, either in theory or through sensory experience, that the Qi — the "universal breath" — is inside us, same as in every point of the universe, that it flows in our bodies, but also enters and exits them without ever completely escaping, knowing that people are immersed in it. **It can then also be understood that the most sensitive parts of the human body allow to perceive this relation consciously.** Different traditions have represented this principle with different images. However, for those who wish to connect the traditions between them, these images can have the same meaning. In Buddhism, we can find divinities like Tara, with eyes on the soles of the feet and the palms of the hands — and between the eyes, the third eye — while in Christianity, Jesus is crucified with nails placed in the same spots — knowing that, at the time, the tortured were nailed at the wrists. Taoism, more pragmatic, prefers to talk about "breathing" through the feet, for example. The martial arts tradition also confirms it, but without actually explaining it for every element of the work. The experience of the practitioner supports it too. Hands should not be closed in the internal work, nor in "standing meditation", nor during slow movements, allowing to receive in awareness, for a long time, the flow of the "substance".

> *A telling example is the form of "standing meditation" called "holding the birds". The principle is to feel the presence of a bird in each hand, by imagining it (but also feeling it!). The work to be carried out consists in tightening the hands, but without*

closing them completely and opening them only slightly so that the birds cannot escape. Every micro-movement is linked to the whole body, obviously. Various other applications are also possible.

Every complete closing of the hands neutralizes the sensitivity of this first receptor. The principle is seen in Buddhist meditation, in the posture of the lotus, with the left hand open toward the sky, the right toward the earth, and the feet soles also toward the sky. Soles that, over time, will progressively "awaken" and, same as the hands, will receive the "breath" in awareness. Henry Plée, "awakener", also stated that open-handed work is superior to closed fists — knowing that it is still possible to work with the fists, but with the principle of "holding the birds". **The second receptor, the soles of the feet**, requires many years of additional practice. **After that, many more years so that one day the whole body can breath in awareness through all of its skin pores.**

It is at this point only that one can hold the bokken like Itsuo Tsuda or Morihei Ueshiba, or the lance like Yue Fei, the "door being open".

Breathing in awareness becomes possible little by little thanks to the work of the Yi — "intention", then "new sense", see the chapter on Yi — which, during the slow movements "kneads the substance", the Qi, to one day make it gaseous; **a state of the Qi allowing the receptors to have the permeability required to exchange, like a "respiration", inspiration and expiration between inside and outside.** Exactly like the zhang zhuang, where work on the relation interior/exterior creates the link with the undivided Qi. **The "transmutation of the body" can thus be completed, thanks to the work done.** However, this requires around twenty years of "proper" work. But before achieving this state, if it comes one day, it is important to understand what characterizes these initial receptors.

The body, an "unconscious" receptor, is naturally in communion with the Qi. The internal work "stimulates" the receptiveness of hands and feet, then body, and in the end allows some parts to also become emitters. The authentic Master is nothing but a "link" between the universal Qi and "the object".

Most of the time, specialists on syncretism pick up drawings of the acupuncture meridians and name the particular points, *"laogong"* for the hand and *"yongquan"* for the feet. But, apart from repeating what has been said and written a thousand times, what is the interest for the practitioner? To be practical, we should try and find the origin of the particularity of these first receptors. Analogically to the work to be done, we can see that to "awaken" the conscious perception in the various parts of the body considered asleep — see "Standing meditation" — it is necessary to "stimulate" them and, subsequently, to establish a feel. The "standing meditation" and the slow movements of the shili kind correspond to this principle.

> *An interesting example. It concerns the interventions of the "scientologist" sect on people traumatized in accidents. The scientologists take turns to massage for hours to "give back life" to the limbs that do not function following this type of psychological shock. This is a "passive" awakening through manipulation. What we are interested in is an active awakening through internal work.*

It is characteristic of a hand to be exerted daily. In our species, the hand distinguishes us — like the apes — and is what has allowed our evolution — together with our neocortex, of course. Consequently, it is the most sensitive area on the tactile level.

The hands are therefore more "awake" — with reservation as to the perceptual numbness of man. The same should be true for the feet, because of their constant contact with the ground, but wearing shoes has diminished, more or less, their sensitivity.

> *I remember being invited to a seminar by Sensei Noro, disciple of Ueshiba. Masamishi Noro asked all participants to massage the feet of their partner. Which surprised me, at the time. Some were even laughing, maybe mistakenly?*

My old Master of internal arts had the habit of looking at the inner side of the arm to gauge the progression of the permeability; "baby skin" equals progress. Note that, despite what was previously said, it is still necessary to stimulate the hands during the first years of practice. They must be put in tension using the fingers, as if they were holding a very big ball, which forces them open. This is to be done during "standing meditation" and "slow movements". Another important note is that the tips of the fingers are particularly sensitive. In the same way, the feet must be stimulated. All done without muscle contraction, which will only lead to a loss of attentiveness.

4. The transmission of knowledge

Today, the transmission happens either regularly, in associations, or occasionally, during seminars, and is open to everyone. The member pays the fee and relies on the group trainings to evolve in the chosen practice, which is the consequence of marketing martial arts as a "product". But, how was it done traditionally? In all authentic traditions, the transmission was done orally and in a discreet manner by "separating the wheat from the chaff". It is often said that it must be done "heart-to-heart". It is always important to understand the significance of the symbols used and, to do that, it is important to ask the right questions. First and foremost, why is the transmission done orally? In writing, a word is limited to its common meaning. However, in some cases, it is necessary to refer to its etymology. But this is insufficient because the social, historical and emotional contexts can vary its meaning. Also, speaking of an "image", all those who have worked with the symbol know that its significance becomes multiple, even infinite, depending on the level of comprehension of the initiated.

That is why the title of this essay is "Guide". Its objective is to indicate a direction.

We are now at the stage where the level of complexity is so high that only those who have experienced the phenomenon described can understand the significance of the text in question. The oral transmission, on the other hand, allows the initiator — if an important reason makes him do it — to bring the useful elements to the recipient in a "live manner". That is to say, not by means of a practical or theoretical method, but mainly by using all the elements of the known senses — sensory — and the unknown ones — supra-sensory.

How could this sensitive relation exist if there were not a symbiosis between the two living creatures who communicate, especially when part of one's experience must serve as Ariadne's thread to the other? A fundamental ingredient of this relation, it is important to remember what Albert Schweitzer deemed to be the most essential quality in a spiritual quest — sincerity. It allows to set aside any relational obstacle, any block toward the "other". This is true for the recipient, who must "open" his receptivity, but also for the initiator, who must "open" his heart in which resides his experience, his awareness. The trust in the other must be absolute, same as in a couple's relationship. This explains the loyalty that must unite the two beings, like a fragile window that can break if one hits it too hard. And if that happens, the appearance of transparency will still be present, but it will not really ever exist again, the trust being now broken. All traditional schools respect the principle of secret and loyalty. In our consumer society this obviously appears utopian.

Standing meditation

Standing meditation: zhan zhuang, ritsu zen.

What could the purpose of standing in a specific posture be?

Physical strengthening; to develop rooting, as some magazines explain with nice drawings; to connect, as a bridge between sky and earth; to make strengthening micro-movements in the six possible directions; to work the small and large circulations of the energy like in all Qi Gong manuals?

When observing a zhan zhuang, all of these questions come to mind. And, it must be said, according to the different existing trends, all of them will receive positive answers. Which will not be wrong and will correspond to the direction given by each practice. They will have their advantages and disadvantages, same as any option offered.

So, we should avoid any comparison or polemic and look at another facet of this work.

First and foremost, the most important part is to state the content of the work. The fact of standing without moving is one thing. Mimes do it perfectly on the street, for hours, and when they move, their density impresses us. Their motor control is accomplished and one might think, logically, that it is superior to demonstrations by experts of the internal arts. Are we to say then that this control in all directions is the objective of the "tree posture"?

The answer is: yes, for the martial arts. At least partially and, depending on the level of personal development, it is but a consequence achieved in a different way, a way whose main objective is to create an awareness of the Qi. It is this *other thing* which is to be found.

What follows is not some theoretical reasoning preceding any practice, nor a synthesis of texts read, but the fruit of personal experience. However, it should be noted that none of it would have been possible without the heritage of the tradition received and without the help of close friends; Masters in internal arts, a Buddhist monk, a Master Yogi, an alchemist and heirs to Western traditions.

To begin with, a short dialogue using an allegory will help to understand the origins of the work to be carried out.

Robert Fludd, *Utriusque cosmi maioris scilicet et minoris [...] historia, tomus II (1619), tractatus I, sectio I, liber X, De triplici animae in corpore visione.*

It is raining today. A calm day of rest. Few things to do, reading and idleness will fill the time. For everything to be perfect, I choose a soft ambient music to accompany this lull. Mozart, my favorite. Music from the heavens, which the recipient has succeeded to express in his score

The hours pass slowly, punctuated by the rain drops tapping on my windows. The pleasant monotony of the lightness of a moment suspended in time.

Listen! This music that I love disappeared from my mind. It is enough that I am absorbed in an activity to forget it. If I read or think, the music does not exist anymore. If my perception is not focused on it, it can disappear.

But if that is true for this example, is it also true for other things, which, with my sensitivity asleep, I cannot feel, perceptions that have disappeared from my consciousness?

Would that be where the esoteric world lies? A world not hidden, but merely forgotten. Forgotten because our field of consciousness has become atrophied, limited, not allowing us to hear the inaudible, to see the invisible, to touch the non-existent, to smell the odorless, to taste what is without taste. Yet, intuitively, I feel that deep inner call which tells me that "it" exists. What exactly? I do not know. At least, while being sincere and not answering with stereotypes read and heard thousands of times, often expressed by people who only repeat something they have never experienced, as always.

Fairy tales or reality?

What to do, whom to listen to, whom to believe, what to trust, my instinct or my reason?

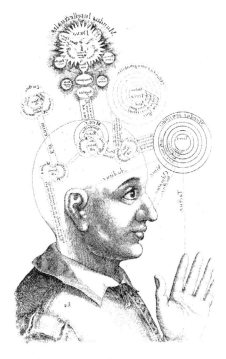

If you are a layman in Qi matters, this intimate dialogue corresponds to the state of perceptual sensitivity you have of the "breath" inside you. Its presence exists, but you do not feel it.

Illusion, one might say! Nonetheless, it is real. I have had students — long time practitioners of external martial arts — from a scientific background, doctors and engineers, who all had this doubt. Which is actually an appropriate behavior, thus avoiding any belief in the miraculous and any subjective perception. These students, as their education had taught them, waited for the result without any preconception, same as in any experimental field study. And so, despite their doubts, they found that the perception of Qi is a concrete fact. But it took them years of perseverance. The lack of patience often hampers the possibility of reeducating the sensitive perception.

So, let us focus on the music that has disappeared from our consciousness.

The obvious question that comes to mind is : "How to awaken this sensitivity?"

Zhan zhuang answers this question.

We must stop fussing, both physically and mentally. Exactly like in chan or zen, where practitioners are told to empty their minds.

Beautiful principle, but extremely difficult, with our brain speculating incessantly and this, even if we decide not to. Which means that willpower is of no use here. It also cannot allow you to feel the "breath". So, stop using it!

You must "fool" your deep brain or, more precisely, make it accept something it does not want : to go on the path where the notion of individuality itself, of separation from what surrounds you, is questioned. And your reptilian brain cannot accept this hypothesis. Its function is survival and you are going where your perceptual "bubble of individuality" is called into question. So, it does its job.

But, whether the hypothesis is accepted or not, it will not help you advance.

What does the Tradition say?

1st step

Stand in the specific position, the so-called "tree" or "post".

- Feet parallel or almost, very little tension
- Legs slightly bent
- Pelvis suspended, no forward or backward tilting — lumbar curvature
- Belly relaxed
- Spine straight, extended

- Shoulders relaxed, low
- Hands open, fingers spread and tense, middle finger salient, wrists bent. Palms facing the body, at chest level
- Arms bent, elbows "falling naturally", like holding a ball against your chest with its internal pressure forcing you to hold it the other way too
- Back rounded, following the curve defined by the arms, with the chest relaxed and slightly concave — *curvature sternum/ shoulders*

- Head straight, in line with the spine, chin slightly tucked in, mouth lightly open.

It is necessary to make the posture alive. It should not be frozen, lifeless. You must feel as if you were suspended by a thread attached to the crown of your head. "**The whole body is like the grass in spring, which shudders, skimmed by an inflow, animated by something unknown**".

The above concerns the corporeal attitude. However, without

the work of the Yi, the previous lines would be nothing but a nice theory, sadly! a bit empty.

The first thing to do is V.l.T.R.I.O.L. This principle is not part of the Chinese tradition, but I am using it on purpose. All traditions share the same essence and leaving "one's church" avoids any tunnel vision or cheap exoticism.

So, "V.l.T.R.I.O.L. — *Visita Interiora Terrae Rectificando Invenies Occultum Lapidem* is a universal alchemical formula[1], which means:

"Visit the interior of the earth, and by rectifying you will find the hidden stone."

For us, martial arts practitioners, it can be interpreted thus:

"Visit the interior of your body and you will find the hidden Breath."

And this is what someone meditating should do in the first place. Visit in awareness the interior of the body.

The first issue is that contemporary people are aseptic and have lost a big part of their animal nature. Shocking? Well, let us define what is the perception of the body for the ordinary person.

Of course, when a pain appears, its placement will be indicated to the mind through a communication by the nervous system. It is the same during a massage. **However, in the opposite case, everything is asleep. Even the hands, one of the most sensitive areas of the skin, will only become alive when in contact with a surface. The need to look in a mirror to verify posture, gestures, as it is recommended in the martial arts, is the result of this common state** — in contrast, in the internal arts, "it is the proper state of mind" which must be applied so that "your spirit becomes substance and that substance becomes your form".

The solution would be to use your Yi, but at this stage this "sense" is not yet usable. **The tradition has found as a solution to physically stimulate the body, so that the brain can receive information about the "presence" of the concerned area.** The various zhan zhuang have as their function to awaken different parts of the body. This is why the limbs, the extremities, the spine, the pelvis, are subjected to a very light isometric tension. To draw a parallel, same

---

1. From Paracelsus, alchemist of the Renaissance.

as the doctor can verify with a pinwheel that a limb is connected to the nervous system, the meditating person can become aware of the different areas of the body by applying light tension to them.

It is therefore necessary, first and foremost, to be mentally present and to consciously visit the body as if it was empty: hands, arms, torso, hips, legs and feet. And then, to connect them perceptually, if possible.

This is the first step and it is important. A big advantage, this "visit" will help you to avoid speculating on various subjects, which your unconscious is forcing on you. Your mind will be busy.

Additionally, to improve said perception, it is necessary to increase your "Jingshen". This notion is discussed in the present guide, but for the time being you should limit this principle to your vitality. Increase your mental influx through the "sensitive image" you want, positive of course. A lived image, like a magnificent sunset or the birth of your child; in short, everything that can exalt you without making you agitated. The agitation presents a mental "frequency" that opposes the perception; on the contrary, extend time, forget it, be aware. Then maintain this state, but let go of the image you "created".

For a long time, the following *preliminary work* must be done before any zhan zhuang. It is intended for those, and they are a majority, who "do not feel much". Perform micro-movements in wholeness, without too much tension, which will awaken your perception. These micromovements must be done with a strong intention, or induction, but with a weak muscle "response", as it is advised in the stage "testing the force", therefore in wholeness.

An important point that is often forgotten: it is necessary to practice in front of something. Most often a wall, but it can be a tree or any other "referent". Stand two to three meters away maximum. The desired effect, which varies with the level of advancement, consists in focusing the Yi on yourself, so as **to avoid "spreading out" mentally**.

Leonardo da Vinci said on this topic that the mind was getting lost in the vast rooms of the castles. It is not surprising to find out that contemplative monks withdraw in cells, in part because of this necessity. But the actual reason is unimportant, trust in the Tradition is needed. The experience will confirm this assertion over time.

With time passing, the Yi improving, the Jingshen heightening, the substance coming into awareness, a certain pressure appears:

- It begins in the hands;
- After some time in the arms;
- Later on, in the chest;
- And lastly, in the legs and progressively the feet.

The feeling is that of the famous tubby Michelin man, inflated with air. This pressure is the first perception of the "substance", the breath, the Qi. It is important not to anticipate anything. Your unconscious not wanting to follow your path and your possible lack of taste for effort will make various sensations appear, an array of illusions, an obvious pitfall.

So, practice, and if the perception appears, accept it, but do not focus your attention on it. It will only limit your future progression, knowing that any attention fixed on a perception, or on a specific point of the body, narrows the potential evolution to the limit thus defined. It is an issue of **the Yi becoming solidified**.

For that reason, even the notion of "Dantian" in Chinese, or "hara tanden" in Japanese, this energetic centre over which practitioners of the martial arts obsess so much, should not become a fixation in your mind. This is a common mistake mentioned abundantly in many works. The centre exists, as well as others, but awakens naturally by following the traditional progression. Here again, we find the frequent syncretism.

The Tradition is clear, not to anticipate anything, not to attach the mind to anything, the Yi and the Jingshen are enough. We are encouraged to let go.

2nd step

If you have followed the previous advice, you begin to feel a pressure, to a greater or lesser extent, inside your body.

The next step is a preliminary to the more fundamental work. It consist in continuing the same work, but in the position called "santi shi". A more "martial" stance, of combat.

- One leg in front of the other.

- Back leg very slightly bent at 30° relative to the front one;
- Hips slightly tilted forward, ready to tilt backward, tense but flexible—lumbar curvature;
- Front foot at three foot lengths from the back one and centered on it, heel a few millimeters above the ground, ready to advance, leg lightly bent;
- Body weight distribution, 70% on the back leg, 30% on the front one;
- Torso, three-quarters;
- Front arm bent forward, back arm bent toward the chest, palms toward the chest with fingers tensed as previously described. Elbows down.

And always:

- Back rounded, following the curve defined by the arms, with the chest relaxed and slightly concave—curvature sternum/shoulders;

- Head straight, in line with the spine, chin slightly tucked in, mouth lightly open;

As can be seen in both examples, the hands face the body. The hands, first receptors of the "breath", are also emitters — see "Emitters".

Placing your palms toward yourself, same as magnetizers do, increases the presence and awareness of the substance that is inside you. Given the level of your Yi at this stage, it is too soon to direct them outwards.

> *As an expert in taiji was saying, badly informed on the following stages of the practice and criticizing the zhan zhuang of dacheng chuan and yi quan: directing the palms outwards for a long time is emptying the substance inside the meditator. But, he was forgetting an important "detail". I will be more explicit in the next stages.*

You are always in front of a wall or a tree, two or three meters away. Your Yi allows you to be aware of your entire body. Eyes on the wall or the tree.

3rd step

Finally! The presence of the "substance" manifests in you. Unfortunately, still not permanently in *everyday life*, but only when you do zhan zhuang or "slow movements with Yi". The substance is in awareness, more or less, depending on the area, and varies in density depending on the day. This is normal because, before reaching a certain level, it comes, goes, comes back and one day stays. Every evolution follows this principle. It is not you who decides!

At this stage it is possible to take the next step, which consists in linking yourself with the object. This is the fundamental internal/external work of the practice of internal martial arts — which, by the way, can be found in all esoteric traditions around the world. The da cheng tradition states: "If you only search inside, you will not find. If you only search outside, you will not find either".

So, what to do? We should remain pragmatic. No need to go back to reading texts explaining how to become "One" by meditating.

> *Also, from experience, to become One cannot be considered an "achievement", but rather to dissolve oneself, to disappear individually, to one day "die while alive". This is also the state of*

«Fana» sought by the Sufis. But we are not there yet.

Concretely:

To a greater or lesser extent, you perceive inside yourself a "substance" that carries you and interconnects the body. This "matter" is not an illusion because you can prove *to yourself*, with a partner, that using it allows you to surpass your own abilities. At that point, it is useful to change to another zhan zhuang, with an induction directed toward the exterior.

The first to be advised is "holding the baby", meaning:

- One leg in front of the other;
- Back leg very slightly bent at 30° relative to the front one;
- Hips slightly tilted forward, ready to tilt backward, tense but flexible — lumbar curvature;
- Front foot at three foot lengths from the back one and centered on it, heel a few millimeters above the ground, ready to advance, leg lightly bent;
- Body weight distribution, 70% on the back leg, 30% on the front one;
- Torso, three-quarters;
- Front arm bent forward at roughly 60°, hand open and perpendicular to the ground, fingers spread and tensed toward the "object" — referent — thumb centered on the face, like a "gunsight".
- Back arm positioned the same way, distanced by one hand both to the side and the back, fingers the same, palm facing the other arm;
- Elbows falling naturally.

And always:

- Back rounded, following the curve defined by the arms, with the chest relaxed and slightly concave — curvature sternum/ shoulders.
- Head straight, in line with the spine, chin slightly tucked in, mouth lightly open.

But the most important in this position is to extend the "substance" inside you toward the object — referent. As you can see, this is where the paths diverge. Some will opt for a tendinous relation, as if there were cables at the tips of the fingers — however, in the "work with sound" no cable goes out. Nevertheless, this "image of cables" is akin to the Yi.

It is necessary to feel the separation between you and the object as an integral part of your individuality. This must not happen at the level of your imagination, but based on the "substance awareness" that you extend.

Obviously, only time will give the answer.

This extension of consciousness directed toward the "object" is done by means of the Yi. It is connected to the substance, or Qi.

You must also exalt, without agitation, your mental state using Jingshen.

But all of this work is to be done, as the name of this zhan zhuang suggests it, with subtlety. As if you were holding a baby. A vast program.

However, this extension of the Qi:

- Should not make you lose the "substance" inside you, your density;
- And to that end, you should not spread yourself, or empty your "substance" like a spilled jug.

4th step

This step is more martial.

According to the work of "guiding the breath" — see below — the density achieved in the various movements practiced must be verified. More importantly, you must take note of potential weaknesses and missing interconnections specific to certain movements done with the wholeness of the body. It is useful to practice the zhan zhuang corresponding to this objective.

A few examples:

- To "cultivate the force": top-down, back/front, by cutting—wholeness of the body, of course.

Zhan zhuang: "lightning descending from the sky"

- To "cultivate the force": bottom-up, front/back, by cutting—wholeness of the body, of course.

Zhan zhuang: "separating the clouds"

- To "cultivate the force": front/back, top-down, by crushing; and also to reinforce the lower body—potentially, in the case of "overpressure" in the upper body, this position is useful to "connect with the earth".

Zhan zhuang: "taming the tiger"

All these zhang zhuang require the enlightened advice of a teacher, obviously.

Many others exist.

5th step

Through "proper" work and patience, the "substance" has become more fluid. The permeability of the body makes it possible for the practitioner to extend the "substance" toward the "object". At this advanced stage of practice everything comes together, only the essence of the work is important.

The practitioner realizes that all zhan zhuang are identical, from the simplest to the most sophisticated. He then chooses one that corresponds to him and allows him "to find himself".

In the same way, certain movements offer the possibility to work with the "breath", identically to zhan zhuang, for an hour or more. The awareness is not only carried into the movement itself, but into the entire body "in relation" to the exterior.

This is the case for:

Mocabu — "friction" step — of dacheng

Tang ni bu — mud wading step — from bagua

6th step

The breath is permanent, the permeability has become a permanent state.

Notes

- With the notion of force in my text, I mean of course light isometrics, and to let the presence of the substance fill the body and link both together. **The whole must be like "a hydraulic system", which connects the entire body. Then, over time, to become more sensitive, to become "pneumatic", which allows to extend this pneuma toward the object.**

- **The pneumatic state is the one allowing the creation of the perceptive permeability of the body and the increase of emission and reception of the breath.** This requires very subtle work and consequently a corresponding mindset. Working "like a robot" is not appropriate, yet a common error.

- For those interested, this type of work ties in with the Taoist Way: **"Refine the Jing into Qi, the Qi into Shen, to then go** toward the Tao". Which I would translate as: "**Refine the vital essence to animate the breath, refine the breath into awareness, to then go from the individual toward the indivisible consciousness of the Universe**". A long road.

To conclude this chapter:

It seems necessary to insist on the fact that the standing meditation must not be a *routine method*. This is not *training*. **It must be lived fully, at every moment, with Yi and Jingshen stoking it**.

Guiding the breath in the movement

"You have been doing zhan zhuang every day, for at least an hour, for the last three years. I also hope that periodically, during your days off, you have been working the posture for three hours. Very well! The next step can begin!"

This imaginary dialogue is what senior practitioners should have been hearing. But reality is not very far from it; I remember, in the yard of one of those small brick houses in Beijing, this young boy who took position next to me. He had come alone without any noise and had taken the "tree posture". He was suffering from the lack of movement and from time to time was kneeling down, then starting again. No complaint but also no encouragement from the Master. Then he left, an hour later, in the same way he had arrived, discreetly. A good lesson for the adult I was.

Today, the culture is different and this form of asceticism has disappeared. But rest assured, one can progress by respecting what follows: not waiting for three years, but practicing in parallel in a dynamic manner, with a clear coherence in the applied principles. This is, to my mind, where the problem lies today.

To continue:

Once awareness of the Qi has been achieved, to a greater or lesser extent, thanks to a regular work of zhan zhuang, it becomes necessary to be able to use this "substance" in the movement—without interrupting the daily practice of zhan zhuang or ritsu zen.

However, to be precise, it should rather be said that the objective is for "**the substance, the Qi, to become alive and one with your Yi**". Nevertheless, to arrive at this ideal, it is necessary to use the tools appropriate for this accomplishment.

The first one is "guiding the breath".

Let us take the example of the "shili" in dacheng quan.

Shili means "testing the force". This is the basic work that is to be done every day, in complement to zhan zhuang.

An identical principle is found in the following arts:

- The taolu in taiji;
- The different slow forms of hsing i, wing tsun, bagua;
- The "ki no nagare" and certain *preparatory exercises* in aikido;
- The breathing kata in karate goju ryu or uechi ryu.

Only the form changes — the container — the background work being identical — the content.

What may surprise the reader in this list are the breathing kata in karate, as well as the aikido *exercises*. However, reading what follows will certainly help the practitioners of these arts to make the connection or to understand what has been lost.

Firstly, the theory of linguistic amateurs states that "Li" is a "brutal" muscular force, opposed to "Jing" — or Jin — subtle force or "energy".

One could smile at such a definition for two reasons:

- Either because one does not believe in the notion of "Jing", all force being muscular strength. Which is not false, at least partially;
- Or because one has experience and knows that, before obtaining one hypothetical day the so-called "subtle" force, he must first go through the physical muscular force. Which means that it is impossible to achieve "Jing" without having worked, initially and for a long time, with the "Li", although in a particular manner.

The modern so-called internal arts often divide the notion of "Jing" — *Jin* — in several distinct forces called:

- Wai Jing or external *energy;*
- Nei Jing or internal *energy;*
- Tzeh Jing or borrowing *energy;*
- Ting Jing or listening *energy;*
- Tzo Jing or following *energy;*
- Nian Jing or sticking *energy;*
- Hua Jing or transformative *energy;*

- Ti Jing or uprooting *energy;*
- Chan Si Jing or spiral *energy.*

However, as some experts can cite more than thirty, I will stop here, since the list will only create complexity of little use to the work on the essence itself. To paraphrase here what was said concerning the Qi: "Although there are many varieties of Jing, all of them are one Jing." The complexity often arises from the intellect and not from the experiential domain.

The "Jing or Jin", the subtle force, can only be obtained after a very long work, so starting at the end will merely create a comfortable illusion. Logically, the latter will not lead anywhere.

> One might wonder whether the work of qi gong – chi kung – does not correspond, in some cases, to the illusion of experiencing a subjective Qi.

It must be said that as long as the "substance" is not tangible at the level of the body — see Qi, Ki — working on an illusion is not going to produce anything. The zhan zhuang, or ritsu zen, is necessary to open the mind to the presence of the Qi, Ki. This practice then continuous to be useful, for a very long time, to increase the density of the "substance", which must be "palpable" and must become usable, over time. But, as previously said, patience is required, which in this case is an euphemism...

Before addressing this possibility, it must be said that some traditions choose to work with the objective of achieving quick results. Effectiveness in the short to medium terms can be a choice for a multitude of reasons, or a non-choice for others.

In that case, which will not be addressed here, the notion of "what is directed inwards" consists in working in zhan zhuang on micro-movements with internal tension, i.e. movements with a very weak amplitude, only a few centimeters, even imperceptible to the naked eye, with an Yi corresponding to a very ample gestural intention. Arresting the movement is linked to the isometric work of the muscles and to the tendons, which are subjected to considerable stress — the Qi is excluded here.

Two options are offered:

- Either a short tension followed by a relaxation,

• Or a maintained tension with vibrations starting from the spine.

Some will also develop the theory of so-called "deep" muscles.

The progression in this type of shili consists in continuing the muscular and tendinous work, with, in complement, the principles of wholeness of the body and of "non-opening". Different types of shili exist. Each shili works the muscle chains more particularly in specific directions — however, it must be said, the "physical conditioning received" is not questioned in this type of practice.

There are many similarities with the work on the Qi, particularly the synergy of the body segments and the muscular intention/induction, which is where the confusion for many practitioners comes from. The authentic Masters know the difference. The shili, in this case, deserves its name of "testing the force".

The modern breathing kata of gojuryu and uechiryu, taken up by other schools, use the same physical principle, but with a bigger gestural amplitude — the fact of training shirtless can only confirm this physical intent, but has this always been the case?

Let us get back to guiding the breath in the movement.

The "shili" is thus work on the movement, whose objective is:

• **In the short term, to gain awareness of the "substance", in complement to zhan zhuang,**

• **In the long term, to transform the "substance" from solid to liquid,**

• **Then, in the very long term, to make it gaseous, if the work and tools are known and understood,**

• **All while succeeding to use this "substance" in the movement,**

• **So that, in the end, each movement is inspiration and expiration of the "breath".**

But this work is also useful, even required, to learn how to use the body in its wholeness — the linking of the body, over time, should become natural, i.e. kung fu. This wholeness is what was previously described: **"When one part of the body moves, the whole body must move."** Every action must then combine a set of Forces in synergy allowing the mass of the body to act as a whole — the zheng ti — the effectiveness of the internal martial arts practice being related to this principle.

These forces can be detailed as follows:

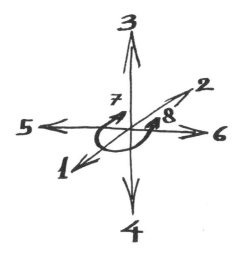

- 1-2: front/back force — or inversely;
- 3-4: high/low force — or inversely;
- 5-6: right/left force — or inversely;
- So, 6 directions — see "Standing meditation".

But the diagram would be incomplete if it did not include rotation, 7-8, allowing to create the useful "momentum". And, as I said, everything should be done in "synergy", that is to say, **at the same time and without discontinuity over the entire set of movements to be performed**.

This should be true for taiji, dacheng, yi quan, bagua, xing yi, aikido and, according to the ancient Tradition, for the breathing kata of karate do, among others.

One better understands the why behind the slowness...

As always, let us take a concrete example: **an action of pushing forward, body forward**.

Depending on the chosen martial art, some elements may vary or may not exist.

- A push with the back leg, back to front.
- The body moves downwards in this action.

- The body shifts to the side.
- The hips rotate to the relevant side.

Everything in synergy.

To that, to be exhaustive, it is necessary to add:

- The role of the back foot;
- The role of the front leg;
- The rolling of the pelvis backwards — and lumbar curvature;
- The action of the spine, stretching and dorsal curvature — some traditions opt for a vertical extension;
- The action of sinking the chest — curvature sternum/shoulders;
- The action of the arms as springs.

If the body goes backwards, push forward:

- A push with the front leg, front to back;
- The body goes upwards in this action;
- The body shifts to the side;
- With hips rotation to the relevant side.

To those must be added the role of the front leg, tilting of the hips, the spine and head positions, as well as that of the chest and arms.

"But how can one push in that last case?" some readers may ask. Well, the inertia of the body's mass and the resistance of the developed synergy must be used, and, at the opposite, the action of the top of the body. To get a feel for this exercise, try it against a wall or ask advice from your teacher.

However, this is only a basic principle, at the least incomplete. It is necessary to associate a feeling of density to the slow movement, even though it must be done in relaxation. Without this density, your movement is empty.

We should not go back to the strong tension that we already excluded. Some, to imitate the density of the Masters of internal arts, use this tension with some visual success. Same as the mimes, by the way, with an obvious demonstrative quality. **But "imitating is not practicing".**

This density must be achieved in a "subtle" way, by using the Yi.

One of the most known ways is the "perceptive imagination". For example, "walking through the mud" or "in the water", "fighting against the wind" or "pushing a piece of floating wood " etc. — the main element to be retained on the level of these images is the notion of permanent perception of the body, or "internal perception", throughout the movement. The last image emphasizes the "subtlety" of the work to be carried out. Indeed, if you push too fast or too far, the piece of wood will escape, too strongly and it will pass above your hands. The difficulty is to associate to it an Yi that goes beyond, a few meters away. So, it requires experience.

But, consistently with zhan zhuang:

- **It is strongly suggested to work facing a tree or any other "object"** — for the "external perception": **wall, column etc., roughly three meters away** — so as to avoid losing your Yi (see zhan zhuang);

- Also, to not forget the role of the Yi, which remains essential. You must **link yourself with the "object" and "bring it into your movement",** using the interconnected wholeness of your body. The presence of the object and the "mass perceived subjectively" will allow you to **"raise awareness of the movement"** (see zhan zhuang).

It could be asked whether In taiji, hsing i, aikido, without the presence of a real "object"-wall, tree-facing the "beginner", it is possible to be aware of the "substance" inside the body and guide it in and out. For an expert, this "presence" is natural on a three meter "perimeter".

With time and practice, the awareness of the "substance" will be effective. This "substance" will offer the practitioner all the useful density he needs and the Yi will be able to guide it inside and outside the body.

A "small" but important detail concerning the progression.

"Everything" becomes natural and any effort to obtain something becomes pointless:

- When the substance carries the body, meaning that it is dense enough to be able to do it;
- When the movement is done through the conscious motion of the substance, the Yi;
- When the connection with the object is real, thanks to the permeability of the body to the Qi—substance;
- When the "substance" is also in awareness on the outside.

Important note: depending on the progress of the practitioner, there is a whole progression in learning the Yi that must be respected — "relation with the object". This progression is outside the scope of this book.

But all of this would be "too simple" if it weren't necessary to also:

"Continue the movement when it must stop and stop it when it must continue.[1]**"**

This obscure phrase means that there should not be any break in the wholeness of the body during series of movements or during repetitions of the same movement. I was going to write "between movements", which would have been a mistake, because there is no "between", that is to say, interruption between movements, **everything must be "one"**.

- This notion must be respected **in the beginning** so that the physical lack of "opening" is also mental — Yi. **The mind follows the body so that one day the body can follow the mind** — the natural Yi and the Qi "guide" the body.

- Lastly, **"non-movement = movement": with Yi and Jingshen maintained, the practitioner is as if "suspended in time"** in a suspended movement. This is a paradox often misunderstood by those who remain in the "physical". It is a state. **Body and mind are one** — as in advanced zhan zhuang.

For example: the front/back and back/front movements of "pushing-pulling" — "or hooking-cutting" — done in series and without interruption. The difficulty will be to not mark a break — an opening — at "the end of the motion", either forward or backward. To accomplish that, it is useful in the "beginning" to view your limbs — and all of the segments put into work — as springs. These "springs" must neither be completely crushed, nor completely relaxed. They must conserve their spring function at each and every moment. Hence, each spring has an action on another — for example: back leg/front leg — the limbs being thus connected together. This must be true for all of the parts of the body in use.

But, here too, this is insufficient, because the theory of "non-stop" — or "non-opening" — at the end of the motion is difficult to apply.

1. Oral tradition.

A reminder: an opening is a "flaw in the conscious presence", which allows the adversary to enter your movement. But, more importantly, it is a flaw in your work with the Yi.

For a long time the non-opening requires a concentration effort from the practitioner to be "here and now". But when the substance is alive, the "here and now" is natural.

The only way is to find the proper coordination between your Yi and the movement, so that one does not allow the other to create a mental opening. The phrase: "Continue the movement when it must stop and stop it when it must continue" provides the solution. Search and you will find. A hint, however, "do not lose the object".

This can all be summarized by saying that **if you make a "thousand uninterrupted movements" of "pushing-pulling"** — or "hooking-slicing" — for example, **it must be felt and done as a "single movement"**. However, paradox par excellence, "**every movement must be unique**". Only experience can clarify that.

It is sometimes useful to take "everyday life" examples, even though the following one belongs to the past. A villager mowing with his scythe is in a natural movement, ample and "sliding", without disruption or rushing, and his movement is done without opening. At each step, the grass is cut, nothing remains. A scythe can be dangerous, so the "presence is therefore necessary", same as it is for you in "testing the force", that is, in the martial arts.

Moreover, to be able to evolve in the practice and approach in the future the notion of footwork, it is important **that there be no "posture" in your practice.**

What is meant by "posture"?

In the modern martial arts, these are positions in which the supports do not vary and remain static. For example, the mabu in taiji, as it is understood today, with the idea of rooting in a motionless state, or the kiba dachi in karate.

This type of error is often translated as "double support" and sometimes as "double emphasis" — which are definitely bad translations.

To address this notion at the sensation level, it is essential to physically perceive each position as fluctuating and an "intermediary toward something else". This is related to the mental state.

Lastly, something that should be emphasized about the physical principles: **the interrelation that must be created between the upper limbs, as well as between the lower ones, and then, one day, between all of them**—all while remaining whole, of course. When you act, the limbs must be "linked" between themselves, in a soft way, as if the action of one is being felt by the other—with a bit of isometrics in the beginning. Then, progressively, to feel that the action of one has an actual effect on the other. And thereafter, with practice and work, the motion of the lower limbs will interact with the upper ones, independently, but in harmony. A paradox that can only be understood through practice. Of course, the objective is to awaken the perception—awareness—in every part of the body.

Afterward, as the Qi develops, a natural "magnetic" interconnection appears—like the one existing between the poles of a magnet. In the martial arts, it is obvious that the ambidexterity of the upper and lower limbs is highly desirable. In the internal martial arts, the essential synergy must be added to it.

Note: In regard to the awareness, this principle also has an impact on the spatial perception (this is related to the cerebral hemispheres). We advise you to refer to the specialized literature on this subject for more information.

But, the most important is, as always, understanding the principles used, which will allow you to work "properly". I know that I am repeating myself, but it is for a good cause, yours. **The objective** is not to perform attractive movements, which copy those of the "grand masters", but rather **to step out of a physical and mental conditioning.**

The classic mistake is to reproduce the stereotyped thoughts of the Far eastern traditions. The latter have been created with the same objective as the Western ones. They are based on the limits of the average person, discursive and logical, and their aim is to provide useful social bases. Only the cultural heritage differs. But, because the exotic aspect is consistent with our conditioning, they can be very attractive.

What is this conditioning?

Like any good self-respecting mammal, we must "enter the herd".

I will not develop again the theory of the triune brain. Instead, I will talk about the notion of "Force". **The one we are using most of the time is the result of the will and a muscular response. Logically, if we want to increase this force, it is "enough" to increase our muscular capabilities**. Gymnastic exercises and fitness exist to that effect. All of our childhood is based upon this type of learning. **Hence, we are programmed at the level of the deep memory to respond to any physical demand through the inculcated pattern**.

Our Western culture can be used as an example: an inflated chest and a flat belly for those who do a physical activity or who want to be liked. Things you should not hold onto in your internal art practice.

Most fighting sports and modern martial arts are based on this principle, as evidenced by the warm-up exercises preceding any training—equally true today for taiji, aikido and many other so-called internal arts.

Are we aware of that? Of course not! As with balancing a bicycle, which, once learned, becomes natural. It is the same for the notion of effort, which can only induce a muscular response. By the way, this is the reason why many refuse to accept any theory of the Qi.

Those who doubt that another possibility exists should test physically a small, or even slender, person, but who really has kung fu. His density and ability can only surprise them, muscular force not being able to explain the phenomenon on its own.

Thus, to find the correct path toward the use of a different "force", it is important to follow the **reeducation of the Tradition.** Reeducation implies slowness, subtlety and, especially, patience... To that end, "tricks" have to be employed for a long while, a term that could make smile, but is nonetheless very apt here. **However, it must be said that the one who should not be "tricked", is "oneself".** So, the proper question to be asked is: **how to escape a conditioning—or, if you wish, a brainwashing**. Or else, how to recreate another by influencing the long memory, so as **to gain access to the deep brain?**

Today, we know that we have to:

- Act on the emotional;

- Go through trying conditions: exhaustion, lack of sleep, of food, or, to put it otherwise, suffering and abstinence;

- Accept daily repetitions to the extreme for a long period of time;
- Avoid reflective thinking during this work.

And, well, the Tradition has always known that:

- The emotional is linked to Jingshen, practicing in an ambiance of "fellowship" or "wellness" does not work. Exaltation through communion with what surrounds us, or through the use of images, is necessary for a long time. After that, the "Jingshen is";
- The extreme conditions are those of the long zhan zhuang where the mental and physical suffering is present — in the "beginning", that is to say, for long time;
- "Repetitions" mean, at the same time, repeating the same movement for a long time, repeating the practice day after day without fault, maintaining the Yi progressively and continually, and passion for the practice, of course;
- The reflective thinking is excluded because the Yi must guide the movement and this requires your full attention — in the "beginning", that is to say, for a long time.

This is necessary, according to the principles used, to be able to touch the deep brain. However, it is also insufficient, yet again. To "trick" your conditioning, the "force" that must be produced — which is, in fact, little to not at all applicable for a long time — consists in generating a "strong intention" and in response "a weak muscular production", but "sensitive" to the extreme. **The purpose is to create "a lack of production", which our unconscious will try to compensate for by using "something else",** the "substance" that the adult is not aware of.

*Which is not the case for a baby, who develops a surprising force, and this, without muscle volume. **This baby, it was you, hence the notion of reeducation.***

Lastly, what is left is **to sing the praise of slowness** in this reeducation. The force used must be perceived as long, very long. You must learn to extend time. How? **Usually, the average individual will produce on a movement an intention toward the goal** of his action. **He will be aware of the beginning of the action** (intention) **and its end** (objective). **Between the two, nothing, empty**

consciousness, with only two points of reference: beginning and end. The same goes for walking. In the military, the "one, two" is a good example: one! two! Each step is hammered on the ground and between the two, empty consciousness. This reminds a bit the modern martial arts: *"ich! ni!"* in Japan, *"yi! er!"* in China...

> *Regarding the notion of "emptiness" in chan or zen buddhism, or the "no-thought", it should be mentioned that the sought after "here and now" is consistent with the proposed work. Accessing it is made concrete by the nature of the "substance" used and ties in "actively" with the theory, so often developed and repeated, of full "passive" awareness.*

Another example, a punch: there is the start and then the impact — or kimono that slaps — between the two... This is why there is an opening when the objective is not reached and especially during the trajectory.

Therefore, in the work to be carried out, the opposite is asked, that is to say, presence extending the entire length of the trajectory — but also, a before and an after without breaking the presence, the "before and after" then disappearing. **The slowness will allow to be in awareness all along the movement. But on one condition, as in zhan zhuang: by stimulating all of the relevant parts of the body**, or the whole body thanks to the interconnectedness.

An example for those who do not have this type of experience: a slow bench press. The muscle exertion raises awareness of the movement (same as swimming slowly in breaststroke).

The difference in the internal martial arts is **the Yi, intention, imagination, together with the "substance", which is the means used for the stimulation.** However, in the "beginning", the density of the "substance" is insufficient to allow the perception of the entirety of the movement, hence the images used and the importance of imagination.

For an expert, the presence of the "substance" is awareness, which is to say "non-opening" without effort of attention, either "in the movement" or "without moving".

However, for a long time, the effort of attention will allow to awaken that which is asleep because of the long conditioning received. **The reeducation consists in progressively effecting an awakening** that is both sensory and supra-sensory — Qi.

The objective is to transform the substance inside you, from a solid state to a liquid one, and finally gaseous, i.e. to open the permeability of the body to the Qi.

To remind the progression already mentioned:

- **The practitioner progressively feels inside him a "hydraulic" force that links the whole body;**
- **Then "pneumatic", more supple, lighter, but still as effective;**
- **And, lastly, a light subtle force that enters and exits like a "respiration".**

Only the last one allows to perform the "fali" or "fajing", the explosive emission of the breath — and not just a clumsy physical action.

There are more advanced levels relating to perimetry, allocentrism etc., but they are outside the scope of this guide.

In short, the work allows to awaken that which is asleep.

You must "regain your baby nature"...

Pushing hands

As time goes on, your surroundings change, transform. Evolution or decay, the analysis is always difficult. On what criteria, depending on what parameters can the judgment be made? Effectiveness, health, spirituality, society, the list can be long. But, whatever the case, it all corresponds to what Lao Tzu said "The only constant is change". A saying, which can also be applied to the internal martial arts where, at every moment, "everything" must be suspended.

However, same as my friend Severin who was my Sempai some fifty years ago, I am constantly surprised by some contemporary aspects of the martial arts practice. More specifically, this surprise is often related to so-called "sporting" events. Indeed, to our eyes, what could be more aberrant in martial arts than modern competitions, where each adversary is trying to find the "hole" in the other's guard to place his technique? To do that, they hop in place, turn, swerve, advance, step back, feign, while waiting for the fault. It is true that these are shows that have to last, the drama being more important than effectiveness, which is not necessarily spectacular, even probably confusing to the untrained eye. These sporting performances of so-called martial arts are only bland copies of a sport that demands courage and skill, the "noble" art or boxing, also called "fist fencing". But is that the correct term? In ancient fencing, both hands were used, one holding a sword, the other a dagger. "Special" moves were the norm, like the Coup de Jarnac, which consisted in severing the tendons of the hamstring. But today fencing also is a show and one has to hop.

I remember how, when I was child, my 70-year-old Master of arms was giving two-hour lessons without weakening and without hopping, lessons whose foundations were close to the karate attacks we knew, Severin and me, at our beginnings. So, where is the issue precisely, the difference? Rest assured, my answer will not take as a reference, like an elderly harping on about times past, the practice of that time, even though today it seems more "correct" to me. Indeed, this is not about nostalgia. I will rather emphasize the foundations of the opposition in the internal arts. They can be condensed in a principle, regarded as a secret in the martial arts. What is that secret? It is "simple", **you must become One. One during the contact of your own reaction with the action of the opponent, be it a punch or a throw:**

- Either he attacks and I deflect, and, "in that time", that is, without opening, I act. Everything in "one motion" including the *ad hoc* footwork. **And, by making the adversary lose his support, if possible** — creating a mental "opening" in him — I avoid any possibility of a follow up on his part;

- Or I decrease the distance and voluntarily enter in contact with the adversary's arms and, in the same manner, I act.

Of course, there is the anticipation, the irimi, the sen no sen, the dodge and retreat etc., but that is another topic.

This principle calls into question any action that requires two times, like:

- Block, counter, so two times — very frequent in martial arts. This never works on a quality adversary. He will never wait for your reaction while remaining static;

- Grip, throw, so two times, for the same reasons.

No need to talk about the hopping...

But, as always, everyone can choose.

If you find this to be obvious, it is either that you have already worked it, or "you are very talented", or maybe you do not see the difference; which is also possible.

Being One in that way is similar to making "a single movement". So, it must be learned beforehand how to execute "series of the same movement", or "series of movements", without opening, in wholeness — see "Testing the force". Otherwise, I am afraid that without this "knowhow" the feeling of being One may only be an illusion. If you are in doubt, approach an expert in the field.

What follows is the beginning of the learning of the principle previously described. **It is the next step of "guiding the breath"**, which should only be approached when the gong fu — or kung fu:

accomplishment in a given field—of the practitioner is sufficient. It consists in working with a partner, which is also called, among others:

- **In taiji, yi quan and da cheng: tuishou**, or "pushing hands";
- **In wing tsun: chi sao**, often translated as "exercises to control the energy";
- **In gojuryu karate and taikiken: kakie**, also translated as "sticky hands".

As always, each tradition differs in terms of form. The taiji works the tuishou in one way, the yi quan and da cheng in another. The wing tsun favours a more dynamic form of chi sao—nevertheless the chosen name appears apt. Lastly, goju and taikiken have a very physical expression in the kakie.

However, as I already mentioned, **the principles are important, not the form**.

To simplify the reading, I will only use the generic term "tuishou".

It can be said, in general, that there are two types of tuishou:

- Using one hand: "dan tuishou";

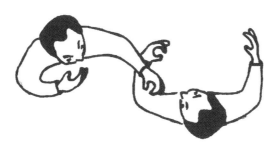

- Using both hands: "shuang tuishou".

Each corresponds to a specific fighting situation. The objective of the tuishou is to improve the kung fu, but also to educate on the martial level, i.e. fight.

- **Dan tuishou corresponds to a situation where the contact with the adversary happens on the outside of his guard** — with an adversary guarding with the left arm in front, you cross his left arm with your left arm, and inversely.

- **Shuang tuishou corresponds to a contact with the arms of the adversary while inside his guard** — and as every fighter knows it, the adversary's back arm cannot be left uncontrolled, hence the usefulness of the tuishou using both hands.

However, in both cases, both arms are to be stimulated. In fact, in dan tuishou, the arm that is not "active" must always be ready to perform a defensive or offensive action.

Numerous techniques of this type exist in every martial art. In short, your ambidexterity has to be "awake", see next — and any position shifting movement must also be possible.

But before all of that?

As I already indicated, **this work must be started when the level of the practitioner allows it. Indeed, how would it be possible to work properly with a partner, respecting the wholeness of the body, the oneness of body/mind, if that were not yet the case when working alone?**

This seems so obvious that it should be impossible to miss. Yet, it is not respected today at all because, modernity obliges, the member of a school wants to learn everything quickly and in an entertaining way.

The best example is the sport tuishou where practitioners are taught to work in opposition too early. This is not consistent with a progression in the internal arts but, exactly like in sport judo, with techniques to make fall or to push outside of the game area.

The problem is that the method used, made of brute force, is opposed to any "internal" progress. The reason for this is simple and logical: it is deconstructing the "reeducation" that is supposed to be happening — although it is also true that it might not have even begun. Additionally, as will be seen later on, the useful "sensitive subtlety" of the practice is lost, where every "mistake" by the opponent should allow a hit. In these bouts, the expression "Four liang (Chinese ounce) push back a thousand jin (Chinese pounds)" is out of place. This is not to be criticized though, the positive aspects of any sport are after all present. It is simply another side of the practice.

Let us get back to the "proper" progression in the internal arts.

It may be considered that the proper level of gong fu means that the "substance" is present, allowing to move in wholeness, without the need to pay too much attention to the preciseness of the movements. Indeed, how can one be able to listen to the other, if one is still paying attention to his body or the Yi? Unless, of course, one moves without being aware of himself, a consequence of the physical conditioning received.

As a reminder, the Yi of the beginner requires attention and therefore the movement itself must be forgotten at the level of technical correctness. And it is a big step to go from that to paying attention to the other...

Nevertheless, an interesting solution is available to the beginner. It consists in being guided in tuishou by a senior. The latter will guide the proper movement and density. The test allowing to see whether you are ready to tackle this level of practice is simple:

- You perform alone, in "testing the force"—*shili*—the movements corresponding to tuishou. It must be correct in quality, meaning dense, whole and unified in action; with or without shifting position;

- And if, according to what the tradition says, **you are capable of being consciously aware of an imaginary partner thanks to your imagination**—without losing your Yi—only then you can begin this practice!

As you can see, this is not a beginner's game.

How to approach the tuishou? Depending on how much practice one has with tuishou, the usefulness of this tool varies. The learning progression can be defined as follows:

- **First and foremost, it allows to be in contact with the partner without losing the wholeness of the body**. And this, in simple movements without resistance.

Reminder: a partner does not resist you and participates in your progress, he only opposes your action in a defined frame, whereas an adversary is an obstacle.

It is to be noted that, and this is from experience, the practitioner who feels the substance inside him and thus the density of his movements thanks to his Yi — after several years of practice — loses partly the acquired abilities when entering in physical contact with a partner. The "why" will be explained later on.

The progression of gong fu is as follows: alone without moving, then alone moving but without shifting position, then alone moving with shifting, after that with a partner, lastly with an opponent.

So, forearms crossed with those of the partner — or hands in contact with the forearms — **the practitioner will have to learn to be One with the other** and this, in a precise gestural definition. Without shifting position, obviously.

- **Next, the practitioner must develop** the so-called "listening energy". But given our pragmatic approach, we will call it simply **"awareness of tactile perception"** — we see here again the notion of "receptor".

  Without losing his Yi — given that the wholeness of the body has been acquired — the practitioner must feel through his forearms — or hands — the variation in the direction of those of his partner. Also, according to the determined work frame, he must eventually vary the direction of his own forearms without losing contact with the partner.

This notion of "tactile listening" is essential in the martial arts. Those who think only about "sight" forget that the sense that allows reacting immediately is the touch. Burn yourself and you will see! The instinct knows perfectly well how to use this sense, which is essential at short distances.

It is necessary to transmit the wholeness of the body to those two forearms — or hands — as well as to perceive any weakness in those of the partner. I remind, at this stage, the work is done in "harmony".

- In the same way, the practitioner must awaken the perception of the arm — or hand — that does not correspond to his "manual preference" — left side if right-handed and vice versa. **The ob-**

vious objective is to develop ambidexterity, rather important in the martial arts.

- When the level is adequate, according to the previous definition — that is to say, working in harmony with a partner is of equal value to working alone — the next step can begin. It consists in performing the same work but while moving around — obviously, it is implied that the practitioner is able to do these movements with a proper kung fu.

But this work in tuishou when moving around must also be done in harmony. Each one being able to "imprint" the direction of their movement, the other "listening" to any variation; and inversely. In the beginning, in one line, then varying in multiple directions when possible.

There is an important point not to be missed. While "listening" to the other, if the direction of your (his) movements escapes your own "central line", it is necessary to "let go" and not "catch up" to the partner's hand(s). Otherwise it would mean that you are ready to lose your own protection of your "central line" and thus become vulnerable.

- **When everything preceding has been acquired, the next step, contrary to what one may think, is still not opposition, but learning the principles for** (this list is not exhaustive):
- Pull and act in that time;
- Deflect and act in that time;
- Take the central line;
- Make lose support, act in that time;
- Use the force of the other;
- "Feel" the opening, act in that time;
- Create the opening, act in that time.

It is to be noted that the principles can be achieved by interaction through the different techniques of the tradition followed. It is at this stage that the *simple techniques* of "testing the force" find their application.

For example, a punch is not a single action, but the source of multiple ones with the use of the opposite arm and a motion to

engage the whole body, same as for any other technique.

It is possible to give an example:

- In shuang tuishou:

  Zuanquan: in the natural "momentum" of the tuishou, when your back arm "moves back" with the body and is above the opponent's one, the movement of the body must be switched forward, all while screwing this same arm on top of the adversary's one to hit with the fist — and, at the same time, with your front arm, you screw to "suck in" the adversary's other arm — **either on top or under it**;

- Dan tuishou:

  Pao quan: when the adversary's arm moves toward you and your body backs up: your back arm intervenes "in that time" and pulls the adversary's arm toward you and in parallel to your body, inverting his movement, his advance, allowing your front arm to free itself for a hit — the two forces, yours and that of your opponent thus encountering each other.

There are a multitude of techniques to be presented, but their explanations require the enlightened advice of a teacher.

By studying the chosen art in this manner, it is easier to understand why certain "awakeners" of the martial arts have emphasized the aberration of some principles in the modern martial arts, like:

- The "automated" hikite in karate — retreat of the opposite fist when punching, hence the uselessness of that arm in the action toward the adversary;

- The use of gloves — the other arm is at least useful in protection thanks to the glove, but this habit makes it unusable for other ends, which is not the case for bare hands;

- The technical conditioning to static situations;

- Reacting in two times to an attack.

Every tradition has its techniques, but the principles of "listening", "ambidextrous action", "exploiting the opening", "synergy of top and bottom", "being One", "timing offsets — *while being One*" remain always true.

Lastly, by mastering or almost what precedes, working with

an opponent becomes possible.

The gong fu of the practitioner can be evaluated through his dan tuishou. Relative to his "size", the internal arts expert can produce a force unusual for a neophyte. His arm possesses not only the density of the wholeness of the body, but also "something else" that is not understandable.

With a real expert, in shuang tuishou, the sole advance of his leg between yours means that he dominates you and that his action is possible. He does not need to push.

Having had the experience with an aged "grand Master" of the internal, the most surprising is the empty force, "Kong jin". It corresponds to a "non-tangible" force, which cannot be resisted. A possible explanation of the phenomenon could be the absorption of Qi by someone who masters perfectly "the inspiration/expiration of the breath". Which would partially explain the loss of ability of the beginner in his initial tuishou—a weak emission of Qi absorbed by the other and inversely.

To conclude, it can be affirmed that the tuishou, when properly learned, is essential to the martial education of the practitioner. It requires, as always, a "knowledgeable" teacher.

Epilogue

Before concluding, I believe it is necessary to give some advice.

The first one is to "**have an ecumenical perspective**".

Take the example of "our" internal martial art. Most of the time, those who practice it or teach it will initially copy the culture of reference. This imitation will often be caricatural. The legendary Taoist or Buddhist dress will be used, a vocabulary to go with, and the circumstantial attitude. Forgetting that the contemporary authentic Masters do not look at all for the appearances of old, except for a few who compensate a lack of depth with this kind of superficiality.

Avoid picking up periodically this type of paraphernalia, the practice has to be constant in time and natural, without embellishments. It is enough to remind yourself that "you must have the correct state of mind" and this, even in appearance. And mainly, do not limit yourself to recitation of Far eastern texts. Read them, study them[1] but in parallel open your mind to other traditions from any origin and, rather than searching for the differences that some people favor in their development, search for the commonalities. This is essential.

But the most important is that this approach will allow you to encounter other open-minded traditions.

Thanks to this mental attitude, you will be able to see that the elements of the work, which have been entrusted to you, also exist in your own culture and in a surprisingly similar form.

Here are a few examples of this.

- The relation between the Alchemist and the matter, where the quality of his soul complements the operating method. It can be asked whether the Artwork is even possible without that quality. In which case, is not the Alchemist himself in fusion with Everything inside the crucible? Exactly like the Taoist and Buddhist meditation Masters, but also the Greek philosophers

1. Some reading suggestions are given in the bibliography.

or the Western monks in contemplation;

- The magnetizer Filiatre advised in 1906 the following daily work:

  "On the development of the magnetic agent (...) Insert a thread into a piece of paper. Attach the thread with a pin to a door, a wall, or to some piece of furniture, then act like you would do it on the shoulders of a subject and exercise yourself to try and pull the paper toward yourself, thinking intensely that it must follow your hands... First, do not move your hands, then take them away slowly while doing an internal effort as if you wanted to pull the paper toward yourself. Continue this exercise for five to ten minutes, approaching and removing your hands. Do not tense your hands, relax your muscles as much as possible and wish strongly to attract."[1]

The resemblance with the Chinese internal work of Yi is surprising, is it not?

- Other examples of this kind can be mentioned, such as the "mental effort" in hypnosis.

- Sedir, in his essay on consciousness, from the same period:

  "Consciousness is the ability of the self to acknowledge its individualist distinction from other objects; it is the relation established between self and non-self through various systems of sensitivity. Its existence necessarily presupposes that of the ability to perceive... The sages in India thought that mind and matter are not opposite things, but rather the two poles of the same "light"; one of the consequences of this theory lead them to dress the emotions and ideations of the human being in a certain aspect of materiality."[2]

Theory also developed by Papus and other students of the School of Magnetism in Lyon, founded by the miracle worker Master Philippe, whose tradition seems to have been lost.

  The magnetism is the link with the person, the consequence of empathy, that is, union with the other. The work of the Yi, of the intention, the ideation, the "widening of the field of consciousness", are the common points with the internal work in martial arts.

---

1. Jean Filiatre, *Hypnotisme et magnétisme*. Nota: some facsimiles have modified somewhat the original text.
2. Sedir, *Les Miroirs magiques*.

This "resonance" appears to be universal:

- The hatha yoga, art of "spiritual liberation", where work with the breath is omnipresent. The approach proposes the work of the "Asanas", postures allowing, as the Tradition says, to "raise awareness of the breath" and coincides with the zhan zhuang previously described. But also the "Pranayama", breath retention work — and the techniques of hatha yoga in general — which does not have as its objective, as it is thought today, to provoke a physiological massage, clear the organism or vivify the antibodies, but rather to link "the Atman to the Brahman", "the individual breath — the substance — to the cosmic breath" in awareness.

    The parallel between "Asanas" and standing meditation, "zhan zhuang or ritsu Zen" the way I described it, becomes then obvious; and in the same way, the "Pranayama", which guides the breath inside the body exactly like the "shili" or "taolu".

- The "dhikr" in Sufism can also be mentioned, which is work with the sound and breath allowing, according to this tradition, "the liberation of the spirit toward God" through the relation of the internal breath with that external. Or, also the "overtone chanting", named "dbyangs", "vowels" in Tibetan, where two to three notes are simultaneously emitted, as well as the Buddhist "Mantra", "tool of the spirit" in Tibet, where the principle is the repetition of a sonorous and rhythmic formula, which serves to guide the "breath".

For the initiated, the purpose of these three tools, same as for "Pranayama", is to guide the "breath" inside the body and link it in awareness to the undivided breath — but it is true that they are often presented to the layman as a "magical" formula.

This type of work will remind the initiated of the shi sheng — "testing the sound" — in dacheng, but also the norito and kotodoma in aikido, the Kiai — uniting the breath — in the Japanese arts. Only the direction in the beginning differs but, the tool doing its work, the mutation of the operator occurs; except when "the animal inside is not killed" or at least domesticated...

In other fields or traditions, certain texts are surprisingly close to these precepts:

- The apocryphal Gospel of Thomas: *logion 22*: "When you make the two into one, and when you make the inner like the outer and the outer like the inner..."[1] or "When you make the two into one, the inside like the outside and the outside like the inside..."[2]

- Kabir, an Indian mystic of the 15th century: "The pitcher is in the water, water is in the pitcher, there is water both inside and outside; when the pitcher is broken, the water mixes with water. The truth has been unveiled by the wise."[3]

- Laoshi Wang Xuan Jie of the dacheng tradition is more obscure, but still as explicit for those who know how to read: "Nothing is found outside your body, but it would be a mistake to limit yourself to the body. The person who can understand this phrase will discover the secrets of Boxing without difficulty!"[4]

- And we can also add the oral tradition, which states: "If you only search inside, you will not find. If you only search outside, you will not find either."

The list is very long, even too long to be continued. Everyone is free to do their own research.

The second advice is to **"avoid identifying yourself"** either with a teacher or a Master, or an *image* from a legend. This can make us smile; however, how many practitioners of weak constitution reprise the technical model of their teachers, who are physically favoured by nature and who also have an innate *warrior* instinct. This can only be a nice illusion. But the most harmful mistake concerns the "internal" dimension, because imitating the density of the Master will only lead to developing the talents of a mime. This type of exercise, sometimes aesthetic, is nothing but an act of *counterfeiting*, which cannot have any impact on the deep brains; not to mention any "correct state of mind". This literal "animal mimicry" allows to adorn oneself with the attributes of the other, but results only in bland copies. Of course, this is not to be confused with empathy, which is a form of transmission in awareness. The latter allows to perceive the "proper state" of the Master intuitively.

1. http://qnosis.org/naahamm/qosthom.html

2. http://qnosis.org/naqhamm/qthlamb.html

3. Yves Moatty, Kabir: *le fils de Ram et d'Allah*, Editions Les Deux Oceans, 1988. Shrikant Prasoon, *Knowing Sant Kabir*.

4. Wang Xuanjie, *Dachengquan*.

A parallel can be made with the art of painting. A replica-maker can copy an artwork but not create it. Of course, this can be just a stage but it must be surpassed in order to accomplish oneself.

The "senior" practitioners probably remember, with a smile, how the cinematographic trend of Bruce Lee spurred all kinds of "copies".

In the same way, resting on the past "achievements" of an exceptional Master to validate one's practice and identifying oneself to a point of playing an artificial, to say the least, role, is probably not the best path toward personal accomplishment. Yet, this behaviour is rather frequent; we have all known teachers who even take on the accent of their Japanese or Chinese Master during class.

This only adds another mask to one's "persona" ("personare" in Latin: sounding through), which originally referred to the theatrical masks worn by actors, a term later used by C. G. Jung.

Lastly, the third advice is based on experience. It is essential, at a certain stage, to **"leave room for the "Other" in your practice"**. The objective is not to become schizophrenic, but also not to act with the "Self", the *persona*. Forget yourself, your limits, your problems of all kinds, your various disruptive thoughts. Give place to the one who appears during your meditations. Who Kabir, the Indian mystic from the XVth century, presented as: "Him whom I went out to seek, I found just where I was: He now has become myself whom before I called 'Another!'".[1] This is what will allow you "to find yourself" and act "naturally". But only the practice can bring the beginning of an answer.

This brief overview of one of the paths in the internal martial arts is now over. I hope that the information in this Guide managed to both be worthy of interest and give you the references you hoped for. The path indicated is obviously not the only one that can be followed, but I can affirm that it corresponds to an authentic individual Path of accomplishment.

From experience, I know that these last words may sound differently to different people. The choice of a martial art can be purely utilitarian, in which case the accomplishment is the fight. To become more effective in case of an obligation, of a confrontation, to

---

1. Yves Moatty, *op. cit.*

reinforce oneself mentally, to valorize one's own image, are all often at the origin of such a choice. In that case, numerous schools can correspond to this expectation, depending on the inclinations of the person and the available opportunities. Wushu, karate, aikido, boxing, jujitsu, judo, wrestling, penchak silat and others are now easy to access.

The only thing left is to find the "right" teacher who must not only be a good pedagogue, but also a "brother" or a "father" on an affectionate level—this last link is, to my mind, the only one that allows to evolve in and understand the art.

This is often the first reason that forces the layman to enter the internal art. The demonstrated ability of the teacher must appeal to him. The relation size/power must surprise him. The initial motivation is often limited to this.

I exclude here on purpose the contemporary craze for "wellbeing", "search of energy" or so-called "mindfulness".

But then, it is most surprising to observe the progressive metamorphosis of the practitioner. A very slow transformation, over roughly ten years, which shows an increased sensitivity and surprising changes in interests, going from the purely material to the more abstract, spiritual, artistic and humanitarian. The progression develops gently, even unconsciously, without an apparent revolution.

The practitioner has spent thousands of hours linking his internal perception to that external. He thus discovers previously unknown subtle sensitive variations. From "egocentrism" he gradually moves to "allocentrism". "His" world becomes different, the "other"—human, animal, nature or even object—appears.

Indeed, what are empathy and compassion if not a supra-sensory perception of the other? And is not the work done an extension of the perceptual field?

At least, this is my opinion and mainly the conclusion I was able to make while observing the practitioners who accompany me. However, there are many conditions to this metamorphosis. I am not talking about obvious things, such as working in a "proper" way every day, but about the nature of being itself. Nature that must be particularly sensitive, intuitive and most importantly generous. Absent that, the work will be without result. There is no point in working on "allocentrism" one to three hours per day if the rest of the time your mind is small, petty and narrow.

In conclusion

If we accept the principle that art is not only a question of skill, but also an expression of a sensitive, or even spiritual accomplishment of man, then the internal martial arts must tend toward this objective.

Otherwise, if the art is nothing but a kinaesthetic expression of performance, we remain in the notion of methods, strategies, techniques. The latter are perfectly capable of fulfilling the physical utility needed, but do not correspond to the same path.

The current confusion is found where these paths cross.

And I will add:

The path of the internal martial arts is long, very long, maybe even infinite, the horizon moving together with you.

This is, without doubt, what makes its charm...

Bibliography

- Borei Henri, *Wu Wei*
- Chiambretto Michel, *Wushu, ombres et lumière*, Editions Chariots d'Or, 2000
- Chiambretto Michel, *Art et tradition du travail interne*, Editions Chariots d'Or, 2001
- Chiambretto Michel, *Le Troisième Pas*, Editions Chariots d'Or, 2003
- Chiambretto Michel, *Le Souffle sous le sceau du secret*, Le Mercure Dauphinois, 2013
- Dalai Lama and Chan Sheng-Yen, *Meeting Of Minds: A Dialogue On Tibetan And Chinese Buddhism*
- Dawkins Richard, *The Selfish Gene*
- Despeux Catherine, *Traité dAlchimie et de physiologie taoiste*, translation of Zhao Bichen's *Treatise of Alchemy and Taoist Medicine*
- Filiatre Jean, *Hypnotisme et magnétisme*
- *Jung C.G., Man and His Symbols*
- *Jung C.G., Aion: Researches into the Phenomenology of the Self*
- *Jung C.G., Psychology of the unconscious*
- Laborit Henri, *Éloge de la fuite*, Éditions Gallimard
- Laborit Henri, *Decoding the Human Message*
- Lorenz Konrad, *Evolution and Modification of Behavior*
- Lowenstein Tom, *The Vision of the Buddha*
- MacLean Paul D., *The Triune Brain in Evolution: Role in Paleocerebral Functions*
- Moatty Yves, *Kabir: le fils de Ram et dAllah*
- Plée Henry, *The sublime and ultimate art of vital points*

- Pranin Stanley, *Aikido Pioneers — Prewar Era*
- Sedir, *Les Miroirs magiques*
- Stevens John, *Invincible Warrior*
- Xuanjie Wang, *Dachengquan*

Other References

- Alain Resnais, *My American Uncle*, film based on the work of H. Laborit

Discovery Publisher is a multimedia publisher whose mission is to inspire and support personal transformation, spiritual growth and awakening. We strive with every title to preserve the essential wisdom of the author, spiritual teacher, thinker, healer, and visionary artist.

Printed in Great Britain
by Amazon

77323032R00076